The North American Fourth Edition

Cambridge Latin Course
Unit 4
Omnibus Workbook

REVISION TEAM

Stephanie M. Pope, Chair
Norfolk Academy, Norfolk, Virginia

Patricia E. Bell
formerly of Centennial Collegiate and Vocational Institute, Guelph, Ontario, Canada

Stan Farrow
formerly of the David and Mary Thomson Collegiate Institute, Scarborough, Ontario, Canada

Richard M. Popeck
Stuarts Draft High School and Stuarts Draft Middle School, Stuarts Draft, Virginia

Anne Shaw
Lawrence High School and Lawrence Free State High School, Lawrence, Kansas

CAMBRIDGE
UNIVERSITY PRESS

CAMBRIDGE UNIVERSITY PRESS
Cambridge, New York, Melbourne, Madrid, Cape Town, Singapore, São Paulo

Cambridge University Press
40 West 20th Street, New York, NY 10011–4211, USA

www.cambridge.org
Information on this title: www.cambridge.org/9780521787451

The *Cambridge Latin Course* is an outcome of work jointly commissioned by
the Schools Council before its closure and the Cambridge School Classics Project,
and is published under the aegis of the University of Cambridge School Classics
Project and the North American Cambridge Classics Project.

© University of Cambridge School Classics Project 2003

First published 1992
Fourth edition 2003
3rd printing 2005

Printed in the United States of America

ISBN-13 978-0-521-78745-1
ISBN-10 0-521-78745-9

Layout by Newton Harris Design Partnership
Illustrations: Joy Mellor, Leslie Jones, Peter Kesteven, and Neil Sutton

Acknowledgements

Thanks are due to the following for permission to reproduce photographs:

p. 5, p. 78, R.L. Dalladay; p. 39, p. 77, The Ancient Art and Architecture Collection.

Thanks are due to the following for permission to reproduce from copyrighted material:

p. 54, H.W. Garrod; pp. 54-5, E.A. Havelock; p. 55, p. 96, Robert Fitzgerald; p. 55, Barriss
Mills in *The Carmina of Catullus*, Purdue University Press; p. 56, J. Rabinowitz, *Gaius
Valerius Catullus' Complete Poetic Works*, Verlag Golem; pp. 94-5, Rolfe Humphries; p. 95,
C. Day Lewis; p. 97, Allen Mandelbaum; p.109, Bruce Johnston/BMG.

Every effort has been made to reach copyright holders. The publishers would be glad to
hear from anyone whose rights they have unknowingly infringed.

Preface

This workbook is designed to be used in conjunction with Unit 4 of the **Cambridge Latin Course**. A variety of exercises is provided for each Stage:

- exercises consolidating Latin vocabulary and grammar;
- language awareness exercises, mainly involving work on Latin derivations in English and other modern languages;
- exercises testing oral and/or aural comprehension;
- exercises extending and testing knowledge of Classical mythology and the socio-historical settings of Unit 4;
- readings offering not only increased exposure to Latin authors and their works but also opportunities for literary analysis;
- focused questions on each cultural section.

The *Key to the Omnibus Workbook* can be found in the Unit 4 *Teacher's Manual* (North American Fourth Edition).

This *Omnibus Workbook* is a selection of worksheets from the North American **Cambridge Latin Course** Unit 4 *Workbook* (editors Ed Phinney and Patricia Bell), from the NACCP *Unit 4 Treasure Box*, as well as new material created for the Fourth Edition by the Revision Team. As in the Student's Text, readings from Stage 41 onwards are in unadapted Latin.

We would like to acknowledge the generosity of the many teachers who willingly shared their ideas and worksheets with us.

Lastly we would like to express our indebtedness to Fiona Kelly, our editor, for her expertise, patience, and hard work.

Patricia Bell
Stan Farrow
Stephanie Pope
Richard Popeck
Anne Shaw

Pliny goes hunting.

Hunting was a favorite pursuit of the Romans on their country estates. In the following letter, Pliny writes to his friend and fellow-writer, the historian Tacitus, about his own surprising day's hunting. Read the passage and answer the questions which follow.

rīdēbis, et licet tibi rīdēre! ego, quem bene cognōvistī, aprōs trēs – et pulcherrimōs – cēpī.

    "tū ipse?" inquis.

    "ego ipse," respondeō.

    nōn tamen necesse omnīnō erat mihi ab inertiā meā et quiēte   5
discēdere. ad rētia sedēbam; erat in proximō nōn vēnābulum aut lancea, sed stilus et pugillārēs. mēcum cōgitābam ēnotābamque, ut, sī manūs vacuās, plēnās tamen cērās reportārem.

    sed hoc studendī genus nōn contemnendum est; mīrum est ut animus agitātiōne mōtūque corporis excitētur. iam undīque silvae et sōlitūdō   10
silentiumque magna cōgitātiōnis incitāmenta sunt. itaque, cum vēnābere, pānārium et lagunculam sīc etiam pugillārēs tēcum fer! experiēris nōn Dianam magis montibus quam Minervam inerrāre. valē.

omnīnō	*at all*
inertiā: inertia	*laziness*
quiēte: quiēs	*quiet, peace, inactivity*
ad rētia	*by the (hunting) nets, near the nets*
in proximō	*nearby*
vēnābulum	*hunting spear*
lancea	*spear, lance*
pugillārēs	*writing tablets*
ēnotābam: ēnotāre	*note down, make notes*
studendī genus	*kind of studying*
ut	*how*
agitātiōne: agitātiō	*movement, exercise*
cōgitātiōnis: cōgitātiō	*reflection, thought*
incitāmenta: incitāmentum	*spur, encouragement*
vēnābere = vēnāberis: vēnārī	*go hunting*
pānārium: pānārium	*picnic basket*
lagunculam: laguncula	*flask (for wine)*
sīc etiam	*and also, as well as*
experiēris: experīrī	*find*
inerrāre	*wander on*

1 Of what accomplishment does Pliny boast (lines 1–2)?
2 Why will Tacitus laugh when he reads this?
3 In line 7, write down the two Latin verbs which describe Pliny's normal pursuits.
4 What is unusual about Pliny's hunting equipment?
5 If the hunting proved unsuccessful what, at least, would Pliny have to show for his day's activity?
6 From lines 9–11 list the ways Pliny feels that hunting encourages mental activity.
7 What final two items does Pliny recommend taking to a hunt?
8 What is the effect of Pliny's use of mythological allusions (line 13)? Check a classical dictionary, if necessary.
9 Is this a letter about hunting or writing?

35.2   Latin–English Doubles

Answer the questions below. Question 1 has been done for you as an example.

1   Which Latin preposition is part of a fence in English?   post

2   Which Latin preposition is an English term in trigonometry?   _____

3   Which Latin preposition is a long sandwich in English?   _____

4   Which Latin word for *but* is a preposition in English?   _____

5   Which Latin interrogative pronoun is a chew of tobacco in English?   _____

6   Which Latin word for *soldier* is a measure of distance in English?   _____

7   Which Latin word for *so* is a Scottish cap?   _____

8   Which Latin word for *thus* sounds like the English word used to set a dog on a cat?   _____

9   Which Latin word for *so many* is a small child in English?   _____

10 Which Latin adverb meaning *obviously* is used in English to describe someone in his or her right mind?   _____

35.3   urbs aut rūs

*Look at the picture, which illustrates the letter **ex urbe** on pages 2–4 of your textbook. Draw a single line under the words below which the writer thinks are typical of **urbs**, and a double line under the words he thinks are typical of **rūs**.*

ōtium   clientēs   strepitus   ager   basilica   flūmen   cūria   quiēs querēlae   umbra   pompa   gaudium   recitātiōnēs   arbor   fundus dolor   negōtium   avēs

35.4 Audīte/Dīcite

*Fold the page in half so that each partner sees only one column. **A** begins by reading a direct statement. **B** responds by reporting that statement indirectly, making the correct choice from two alternatives. **A** verifies this choice. Then **B** reads a direct statement, and the process continues.*

A

1 aliquandō amīcī mē vīsitant.
  (dīcis aliquandō amīcōs tē vīsitāre.)
2 dīcis tē carminibus avium dēlectārī.
  dīcis mē carminibus avium dēlectārī.
3 Germānī per viās urbis dūcuntur.
  (dīcis Germānōs per viās urbis dūcī.)
4 dīcis cīvēs Domitiānum laudāre.
  dīcis cīvēs ā Domitiānō laudārī.
5 mentīminī!
  (dīcis nōs mentīrī.)
6 dīcis mē in rīpā flūminis iacēre.
  dīcis tē in rīpā flūminis iacēre.
7 versūs Martiālis mē dēlectant.
  (dīcis versūs Martiālis tē dēlectāre.)
8 dīcis eōs ad aulam Imperātōris invītārī.
  dīcis nōs ad aulam Imperātōris invītārī.
9 prīmā hōrā ā clientibus salūtor.
  (dīcis tē prīmā hōrā ā clientibus salūtārī.)
10 dīcis mē ōrātiōnēs audīre velle.
  dīcis nōs ōrātiōnēs audīre velle.

B

1 dīcis aliquandō amīcōs tē vīsitāre.
  dīcis aliquandō amīcōs ā tē vīsitārī.
2 carminibus avium dēlectāris.
  (dīcis mē carminibus avium dēlectārī.)
3 dīcis tē Germānōs per viās urbis dūcere.
  dīcis Germānōs per viās urbis dūcī.
4 cīvēs Domitiānum laudant.
  (dīcis cīvēs Domitiānum laudāre.)
5 dīcis nōs mentīrī.
  dīcis mē mentīrī.
6 in rīpā flūminis iacēs.
  (dīcis mē in rīpā flūminis iacēre.)
7 dīcis versūs Martiālis tē dēlectāre.
  dīcis versūs Martiālis mē dēlectāre.
8 ad aulam Imperātōris invītāmur.
  (dīcis nōs ad aulam Imperātōris invītārī.)
9 dīcis vōs prīmā hōrā ā clientibus salūtārī.
  dīcis tē prīmā hōrā ā clientibus salūtārī.
10 ōrātiōnēs audīre vīs.
  (dīcis mē ōrātiōnēs audīre velle.)

35.5 Word Power: Same Difference

Complete the following analogies with a word from the Stage 35 Vocabulary Checklist:

1 ōdī : amō :: _____ : vērum dīcō

2 iānua : porta :: poena : _____

3 incēdo : ingredior :: cōgitō : _____

4 et : atque :: quō tempore : _____

5 laetus : trīstis :: praemium : _____

Titus Flāvius Stephanus, praepositus camēlōrum

A *Read the story below (about a real person who had an unusual specialty).*

magnus clāmor in portū *tollēbātur*. ē nōnnūllīs nāvibus frūmentum ex
Aegyptō importātum *expōnēbātur*, et ad horrea ā servīs *portābātur*. ex
aliīs nāvibus amphorae vīnī in lintrēs *impōnēbantur*. amphorae ad
horrea vīnāria *vehēbantur* quae proxima erant. ex aliīs nāvibus puerī
puellaeque, catēnīs vīnctī, vēnālīciōs *sequēbantur*. portus ingentī   5
multitūdine *complēbātur*.

   per mediam multitūdinem equitābat Titus Flāvius Stephanus,
Augustī lībertus, praepositus camēlōrum. quadrāgintā servī
Stephanum *comitābantur*. quī, cum omnēs nāvēs onerāriās *perscrūtātus
esset*, ad maximam *prōgressus est*. servī Stephanum *secūtī sunt* anxiī.   10
   ille, cum magistrum nāvis onerāriae *cōnspicātus esset*, prōnūntiāvit,
   "ego sum Titus Flāvius Stephanus, Augustī lībertus, praepositus
camēlōrum. dominus noster spectāculum splendidissimum in Circō
Maximō paucīs diēbus dare vult. ego igitur ad portum *prōgressus sum*
ut quadrāgintā camēlōs et quīnque elephantōs, quī ex Aegyptō *missī*   15
sunt, ad Urbem dūcam."
   "pessimī erunt lūdī!" respondit magister nāvis. "quīnque tantum
camēlōs et ūnum elephantum trānsportāvī. nam praefectus Aegyptī
iussit mē ingentem obeliscum impōnere atque hūc trānsportāre. itaque
camēlī elephantīque cēterī in Aegyptō *relictī sunt*."   20
   Stephanus īrātissimus magistrum nāvis vituperāvit, magister
praefectum Aegyptī.
   intereā quīnque camēlī elephantusque ā servīs *expositī sunt*. ubi
Stephanus ūnā cum servīs animālibusque ad Urbem *proficīscēbātur*,
magister nāvis magnā vōce, "vīsne," inquit, "obeliscum quoque ad   25
Urbem portāre? nam māne ē portū nāvigāre dēbeō."

8

"ego sum praepositus camēlōrum," inquit ille. "mihi nōn licet obeliscōs portāre. māne nūntius ad Diodōrum tibi mittendus est. lībertus Augustī est, praepositus obeliscōrum!"

magister nāvis īrā incēnsus, "cum Diodōrus, praepositus obeliscōrum," inquit, "hūc vēnerit, ego querēlās movēbō!" *30*

Stephanus cachinnāvit. "sī querēlās movēbis," inquit, "Cēnsōrīnō ūnā cum Diodōrō venīre necesse erit."

"quis est Cēnsōrīnus?"

"lībertus Augustī est, praepositus querēlārum." *35*

praepositus	*chief-inspector*
lintrēs: linter	*barge*
horrea vīnāria: horreum vīnārium	*warehouse for wine*
nāvēs onerāriās: nāvis onerāria	*cargo ship*
licet: licēre	*be allowed*
querēlās movēbō: querēlās movēre	*make complaints, complain*

B *Translate each of the verbs below (they were italicized in the story above), and then label them as* **passive** *or* **deponent**.

			Translation	Passive/Deponent
1	tollēbātur	(line 1)	_____	_____
2	expōnēbātur	(line 2)	_____	_____
3	portābātur	(line 2)	_____	_____
4	impōnēbantur	(line 3)	_____	_____
5	vehēbantur	(line 4)	_____	_____
6	sequēbantur	(line 5)	_____	_____
7	complēbātur	(line 6)	_____	_____
8	comitābantur	(line 9)	_____	_____
9	perscrūtātus esset	(ll. 9–10)	_____	_____
10	prōgressus est	(line 10)	_____	_____
11	secūtī sunt	(line 10)	_____	_____
12	cōnspicātus esset	(line 11)	_____	_____
13	prōgressus sum	(line 14)	_____	_____
14	missī sunt	(ll. 15–16)	_____	_____
15	relictī sunt	(line 20)	_____	_____
16	expositī sunt	(line 23)	_____	_____
17	proficīscēbātur	(line 24)	_____	_____

9

Roman Letters

Read pages 16–18 in your textbook and answer the following:

1   What did Romans consider **ōtium** to be? In what two types of activities would Romans engage during **ōtium**?

2   In what four types of activities did Pliny the Elder engage during his **ōtium**? Explain how his nephew seemed to have learned from him.

3   What was the difference between the Greek and Roman worlds that made written correspondence absolutely necessary for the Romans?

4   List eight types of Romans who needed to engage in written correspondence.

5   What would a traveler delivering letters for someone else often receive for his efforts?

6   How would Romans try to ensure that important letters were delivered to the intended party?

7   What five types of items could be found on **cērae**?

8   For what was a **charta** used? Describe its appearance.

9   Of what was a Roman book comprised? What was it called? How was it read?

10 What were **āmanuēnsēs**? Why were they necessary? What were three different Latin names used for the correspondence slave?

11 How would Romans personalize their letters?

12 Who were two of the most famous letter writers in the ancient world?

13 Approximately how many letters of Cicero have survived?

14 With what topics do Cicero's letters deal?

15 What is the main difference between Pliny the Younger's and Cicero's letters?

16 What do the letters of Cicero and Pliny show about their education?

17 List eleven genres of ancient literature. Which two are distinctively Roman?

18 What are three conventional parts of Roman letters?

19 Give the meanings of the following abbreviations or terms: **SAL**, **SD**, **SPD**, **SVBE**, **valē**, **cūrā ut valeās**.

20 What is the epistolary tense?

21 What two common stylistic characteristics do Roman letters share?

22 Why did Pliny recommend letter-writing as a valuable area of study?

23 Unlike today, what did publications not provide their authors? What did they provide instead?

poēta vērus

Read the following scene. Then assign parts and perform it aloud.

poēta Martiālis per urbem contendit ut amīcum vīsitet.

Martiālis:	mihi festīnandum est. nam amīcus meus epigrammata audīre cupit.
turba:	(*in forō clāmāns*) caudex! asine!
Martiālis:	heus! quid audiō? putō mē propius appropinquāre dēbēre *5* ut cognōscam cūr illa turba rīdeat. suspicor enim aliquid rīdiculī accidere … et tū, Martiālis, semper rēbus rīdiculīs dēlectāris. (*Iuvenālem, amīcum bonum, cōnspicit.*)
Iuvenālis:	tū opportūnē venīs, mī amīce! iste senex quī in rostrīs stat recitāre cōnātur. tamen, quotiēns recitātiōnis initium fēcit, *10* turba magnīs clāmōribus cachinnat.
Martiālis:	tacē! ille incipit.
senex:	dīcis amōre tuī bellās ardēre puellās,
	quī faciem sine aquā, Sexte, natantis habēs.
audītor:	quō modō potest Sextus sine aquā natāre? hoc epigramma *15* intellegere nōn possum.
aliī audītōrēs:	caudex! asine!
Iuvenālis:	hic senex tam stultus est ut epigrammata tua auferat neque verba intellegat. Sextus sub aquā, nōn sine aquā natat.
senex:	(*recitātiōnem renovat.*) *20*
	Thāida Quīntus amat. "quam Thāida?" "Thāida caecam."
	nūllum oculum Thāis caeca habet, ille duōs.
Martiālis:	satis! satis! hic asinus epigrammata mea dēlet. (*audītōribus*) amīcī! vōs hortor ut mihi dīcere liceat.
audītōrēs:	ecce Martiālis, scrīptor vērus! audiāmus! *25*
Martiālis:	(*senī appropinquat.*) quis es, homuncule?
senex:	(*ērubēscēns*) Fīdentīnus sum.
Martiālis:	tū male recitās, amīce. sed fortasse tū melius recitāris:
	quem recitās meus est, ō Fīdentīne, libellus.
	sed male cum recitās, incipit esse tuus. *30*
audītōrēs:	optimē! optimē! (*tum Fīdentīnum ē forō agitant.*) caudex! asine!

propius	*nearer, closer*
opportūnē	*at the right time*
audiāmus	*let's listen!*

More of Martial's Art

Read the following epigrams of Martial. Then answer the questions.

1 *dē Linō, iuvene foedō*

  quid mihi reddat ager quaeris, Line, Nōmentānus?
    hoc mihi reddit ager: tē, Line, nōn videō.

  Nōmentānus *of Nomentum* (a town in northern Latium)

  What does the adjective **Nōmentānus** describe? What is the return, or profit, that Martial derives from his country property?

2 *dē pauperibus et dīvitibus*

  semper pauper eris, sī pauper es, Aemiliāne.
    dantur opēs nūllīs nunc nisi dīvitibus.

  What English saying matches the theme of this epigram?

3 *dē Polliōne, quī multum bibit*

  omnia prōmittis cum tōtā nocte bibistī;
    māne nihil praestās. Pollio, māne bibe.

  praestās: praestāre *carry out, make good*

  What request does Martial make of Pollio? Why?

4 *dē Philerōte, quī maximās dīvitiās ab uxōribus mortuīs comparāvit*

  septima iam, Philerōs, tibi conditur uxor in agrō.
    plūs nūllī, Philerōs, quam tibi reddit ager.

  conditur: condere *bury*
  nūllī   *to no one* (dat. of **nēmō**)

  Whom does the adjective **septima** describe? Does Martial think Phileros is to be congratulated or pitied for having lost so many wives?

5 *difficilis facilis*

  difficilis facilis, iūcundus, acerbus es īdem:
    nec tēcum possum vīvere, nec sine tē.

  iūcundus *pleasant*
  acerbus   *troublesome*

  Is the contradictory person addressed in this poem a man or a woman?

12

"pe" Words

Fill each set of blanks by rearranging the scrambled letters to make a Latin word which translates the English word in parentheses.

1 pe _ _ _ _ _   strui   (skillful)

2 _ pe _ _ _ _   rresa   (to hope)

3 _ _ _ pe _   shos   (guest)

4 _ _ _ _ _ pe _ _   rimerur   (to burst in)

5 _ _ _ _ _ pe _   shaxur   (soothsayer)

6 _ _ _ pe _ _ _ _   mastest   (storm)

7 _ _ pe _ _ _ _   dirmie   (to hinder)

8 _ pe _ _ _ _   raire   (to open)

9 pe _ _ _ _ _   icanu   (money)

Trellis of English Translations

Fill the squares of the trellis below with English words:

2-letter words for **in, minimē**
3-letter words for **dēbēre, decem, īrātus, sedēre**
4-letter words for **umquam, minus, antīquus, pars**
5-letter words for **numquam, vōx, fēmina, peior, somniāre, dīrus, palluit, septem**
7-letter words for **lībertās, neglegere**

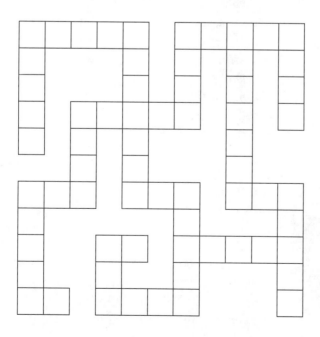

13

Waiting for an Audience

The following passage by Pliny shows that Martial was not the only writer who had trouble with members of his audience. Read the passage and answer the questions which follow.

magnum prōventum poētārum annus hic attulit: tōtō mēnse Aprīlī nūllus
ferē diēs, quō nōn recitāret aliquis. iuvat mē quod vigent studia,
prōferunt sē ingenia hominum et ostentant, tametsī cīvēs audītum pigrē
coeunt. plērīque in statiōnibus sedent tempusque fābulīs audītīs
conterunt. subinde sibi nūntiōs ferrī iubent an iam recitātor intret, an   5
dīcat praefātiōnem, an ad fīnem librī appropinquet; tum dēmum ac tunc
quoque lentē cunctanterque veniunt, nec tamen manent, sed ante fīnem
recēdunt, aliī dissimulanter et furtim, aliī simpliciter et līberē. at hercule
memoriā parentum Claudius Caesar, cum in Palātiō spatiārētur, audīvit
clāmōrem, causamque requīsīvit; "recitat" inquit aliquis, "Noniānus."   10
Claudius subitus recitantī inopīnātusque vēnit. nunc ōtiōsissimus quisque
multō ante rogātus et identidem admonitus, aut nōn venit aut, sī vēnit,
queritur sē diem (quia nōn perdit) perdere.

prōventum: prōventus	*harvest, yield*
ferē	*almost*
iuvat mē	*it pleases me*
vigent: vigēre	*thrive, flourish*
studia: studium	*literature*
prōferunt sē: prōferre sē	*emerge*
ostentant (sē): ostentāre (sē)	*be on display*
tametsī	*although*
pigrē	*slowly*
coeunt: coīre	*meet, assemble*
statiōnibus: statiōnēs	*public places*
fābulīs: fābula	*gossip, anecdote*
conterunt: conterere	*waste*
subinde	*from time to time*
praefātiōnem: praefātiō	*introduction*
tum dēmum	*then finally*
tunc	*then*
recēdunt: recēdere	*go away*
dissimulanter	*secretly*
furtim	*stealthily, secretly*
simpliciter	*plainly*
līberē	*freely, boldly*
Claudius Caesar	*Emperor Claudius* (emperor, A.D. 41–54)
spatiārētur: spatiārī	*stroll*
requīsīvit: requīrere	*ask*
Noniānus	*Nonianus* (a famous orator)

subitus	*sudden*
inopīnātus	*unexpected*
ōtiōsissimus quisque	*every absolutely idle person*
queritur: querī	*complain*
perdit: perdere	*waste*

1 What does Pliny say this year has brought?
2 What has been happening all through April?
3 Why is Pliny pleased?
4 On the other hand, the behavior of the listeners does not please him. List the things that they do which he does not like.
5 What contrast does Pliny draw with the behavior of the Emperor Claudius?
6 What are the last comments that Pliny makes about idle people in his time?

36.6 Snake Sentences

Translate each English sentence into Latin by selecting correctly from the list of Latin words and phrases.

1 **Sabidius is becoming so angry that he cannot reply.**

Sabidius	adeō	īrāscētur	ut	respondērī	nōn possit.
Sabidium	tamquam	īrāscitur	ut	respondēre	nōn potest.

2 **The listeners do not know why Thais has one eye.**

audītor	nesciunt	quō modō	Thais	ūnum	oculō	habeat.
audītōrēs	nescit	quārē	Thaida	ūnō	oculum	habet.

3 **Martial is so astonished by the sound that he stands motionless.**

Martiālis	sonitū	tum	attonitī	est	ut	immōtī	stet.
Martiālem	sonitibus	tam	attonitus	erat	ut nōn	immōtus	stat.

4 **Pliny wants to know why the citizens leave before the end.**

Plīnius	scīre	volunt	cūr	cīvis	post fīnem	discēdat.
Plīniō	scit	vult	quō modō	cīvēs	ante fīnem	discēdant.

5 **Glabrio is rushing to the auditorium to enjoy the poet's verses.**

Glabriō	ad audītōrium	ruit	ut	poētārum	versūs	fruātur.
Glabriōne	ab audītōriō	ruet	nē	poētae	versibus	fruitur.

6 **Women come to the games to see and to be seen.**

fēminae	ad lūdōs	venient	ut	videant	et	videntur.
fēmina	ā lūdīs	veniunt	nē	vident	aut	videantur.

36.7   Word Power

A   *"-ate" is enough. Match the meaning to the English derivative.*

1   denigrate
2   disparate
3   evacuate
4   inveterate

a   not alike or equal
b   longstanding; habitual
c   to defame
d   to make empty; empty the contents of

B   *Off on a Tangent. Write English derivatives from **tangō ... tactus** to match the following definitions:*

1   able to be touched
2   touching but not intersecting (geometry)
3   a dance in which couples touch
4   to get in touch with
5   dependent upon, conditional
6   near; adjoining

16

36.8 recitātiōnēs

Read pages 34–36 in your textbook and answer the following:

1 How might an author first present his work and where?
2 What was Martial's complaint about Ligurinus?
3 Where also (more comfortably) might a first reading have taken place? Who might have been there?
4 How could some hosts make nuisances of themselves?
5 What was a **recitātiō**? For what two purposes was it given?
6 List three places where a **recitātiō** might be given. Describe the setting of the reading.
7 Who paid for the costs of the **recitātiō**?
8 What might an unscrupulous or anxious author do?
9 Who usually gave the readings? For what reason would there be an exception?
10 Describe the recital procedure. How long might it have lasted?
11 What amusing accident happened at Emperor Claudius' reading?
12 Why was an historian asked not to read the next installment of his work? How could this cancellation have helped the sale of the book?
13 According to Pliny, some people behaved frivolously at readings. Describe some of this behavior.
14 Explain how each of these authors viewed public readings:
   a Pliny the Younger
   b Martial
   c Seneca
   d Juvenal

glōria Agricolae

*Below is the text of an inscription which might have appeared on the base of the statue awarded to Agricola and set up in Rome on his return from Britain. As usual, the inscription is abbreviated: the expanded version of each new word is given beneath. The shaded letters indicate words which would have been scraped out after the death (in A.D. 96) and subsequent official condemnation (**damnātiō memoriae**) of the acts of Domitian.*

Read the inscription and answer the questions which follow.

CN IVLIO L F ANI AGRICOLAE COS PONTIF XVIR STLIT IVDIC TRIB MIL LEG VIIII HISP Q PRO PR PROV ASIAE TR PLEB PRAET LEG IMP DIVI VESPASIANI AVG LEG XX V V ADLECTO INTER PATRICIOS AB IMPERATORIB DIVO VESPASIANO ET DIVO TITO LEG PRO PR IMP DIVI VESPASIANI AVG PROV AQVITAN LEG PRO PR IMP DIVI VESPASIANI AVG ET IMP DIVI TITI CAES AVG ET IMP CAES DOMITIANI **AVG GERMANICI PROVINC BRITANNIAE HVIC SENATVS AVCTORE IMP CAES** DOMITIANO **AVG GERMANICO TRIUMPHALIA ORNAMENTA DECREVIT STATVAMQVE PECVN PVBLIC PONEND CENSVIT**

Note: this inscription is in the form: TO AGRICOLA (all his offices listed) THE SENATE … HAS DECREED …

ANI	Aniēnsī (tribū): Aniēnsis (tribus)	*Aniensian tribe*
XVIR STLIT IVDIC	decemvirō stlītibus [= lītibus] iūdicandīs: decemvir stlītibus iūdicandīs	*judge in inheritance court*
HISP	Hispānae: Hispāna	*"Spanish Legion"*
Q PRO PR	quaestōrī prō praetōre: quaestor prō praetōre	*governor's aide*
TR PLEB	tribūnō plēbis: tribūnus plēbis	*tribune of the people*
PRAET	praetōrī: praetor	*praetor*
LEG … LEG	lēgātō … legiōnis: lēgātus legiōnis	*legionary commander*
AVG	Augustī: Augustus	*(a title given to Roman emperors)*
V V	Valeriae Vīctrīcis: Valeria Vīctrīx	*"Valerian Victorious Legion"*
ADLECTO INTER PATRICIOS	adlēctō inter patriciōs: adlēctus inter patriciōs	*raised to patrician rank*
LEG PRO PR	lēgātō prō praetōre: lēgātus prō praetōre	*governor*
PROV AQVITAN	prōvinciae Aquitāniae: prōvincia Aquitānia	*Aquitania (a province in south-western Gaul – modern Languedoc)*
CAES	Caesaris: Caesar	*(a title given to Roman emperors)*
TRIVMPHALIA ORNAMENTA	triumphālia ōrnāmenta: triumphāle ōrnāmentum	*decorations associated with a triumph parade (which Domitian did not allow Agricola actually to hold)*
PECVN PVBLIC	pecūniā pūblicā	*at public expense*
PONEND	pōnendam: pōnere	*put up*
CENSVIT	cēnsuit: cēnsēre	*vote*

18

1 What was Agricola's highest political office?
2 In which three provinces did Agricola serve? What rank did he hold in each province?
3 Under which three emperors did Agricola serve? Who especially helped him in his career?
4 In which two legions did Agricola serve? What rank did he hold in each?
5 Which emperor was given the honorary name Germanicus? Why? (See Unit 4, p. 48.)
6 Which of the emperors was alive at the time the inscription was executed? How can you tell from the inscription?
7 Suggest reasons why Domitian's acts were condemned after his death and his name was erased from inscriptions. Give examples of similar events today.

37.2   Quintus says to Cogidubnus that ...

In the indirect statements below, choose the correct Latin word in each set of parentheses, and then translate the entire indirect sentence.

1 DIRECT: "nāvis ad pharum Alexandrīae pervēnit."
   INDIRECT: Quīntus Cogidubnō dīcit (nāvis/nāvem) ad pharum Alexandrīae (pervēnisse/pervēnit).

2   DIRECT: "mīlitēs Rōmānī servōs turbulentōs comprehendērunt."

    INDIRECT: Quīntus Cogidubnō dīcit mīlitēs (Rōmānōs/Rōmānī) servōs turbulentōs (comprehendērunt/ comprehendisse).

3   DIRECT: "ego et Clēmēns ad templum Augustī Caesaris festīnāvimus."

    INDIRECT: Quīntus Cogidubnō dīcit sē et (Clēmentem/Clēmēns) ad templum Augustī Caesaris (festīnāvērunt/ festīnāvisse).

4   DIRECT: "multum vīnum ā mē in āram fūsum est."

    INDIRECT: Quīntus Cogidubnō dīcit multum vīnum ā sē in āram (fūsum est/ fūsum esse).

5 DIRECT: "ego vīllam Barbillī
             mox invēnī."
   INDIRECT: Quīntus Cogidubnō
             dīcit sē vīllam
             Barbillī mox
             (invēnisse/invenīre).

37.3 The Brave Mauricus

Pliny tells an anecdote about his friend, Junius Mauricus, who behaved courageously before the Emperor Nerva. The notorious informers, Catullus Messalinus and Fabricius Veiento, mentioned in the anecdote had belonged to Domitian's cōnsilium and appear in the fictional stories in Stage 37. By the time of this anecdote Catullus Messalinus was dead. Read the passage and answer the questions which follow.

cēnābat Nerva cum paucīs amīcīs; Vēientō proximus atque etiam in sinū recumbēbat. incidit sermō dē Catullō Messālīnō quī oculīs orbātus ingeniō iam saevō dolōrem caecitātis addiderat. nōn verēbātur, nōn ērūbēscēbat, nōn miserēbātur; ideō saepissimē ā Domitiānō sīcut hasta quae caeca et improvida fertur in omnēs bonōs iactābātur. dē huius   5
sceleribus, vitiīs, sanguināriīs sententiīs inter sē post cēnam loquēbantur cum ipse imperātor rogāvit quid iste paterētur sī vīveret. et Mauricus, "nōbīscum cēnāret."

sinū: sinus	*lap*	sanguināriīs:	
incidit: incidere	*occur*	sanguinārius	*bloodthirsty*
orbātus (+ ABL)	*deprived of*	quid … paterētur	*what he would be*
caecitātis: caecitās	*blindness*		*putting up with*
miserēbātur: miserērī	*have pity*	sī vīveret	*if he were alive*
improvida: improvidus	*unforeseeing,*	cēnāret	*he would be dining*
	unthinking		

1 Whom did the emperor most favor at the dinner? How do we know?
2 What kind of man was Catullus Messalinus? What effect had his blindness had upon him?
3 What is the point of comparing Catullus Messalinus with a spear? What characteristic made him useful to Domitian? And what did Domitian use him for?
4 Of whom in Unit 4 does the character of Mauricus remind you?
5 Why do you think Pliny considers Mauricus a brave man?

mors Agricolae

*Read the story below, based on Tacitus' biography of Agricola, and answer the
questions which follow.*

fīnis vītae eius fuit suīs lūctuōsus, trīstis amīcīs, omnibus bonīs nōn sine
cūrā. nūntiō mortis acceptō, magna multitūdō domum Agricolae cucurrit
ut causam cognōsceret; et per fora, per circulōs omnēs dē morte locūtī
sunt. nec quisquam, audītā morte Agricolae, aut laetātus est aut oblītus.

    multī dīcunt Agricolam venēnō periisse. ego nihil prō certō affirmāre   5
velim; certē ad eum aegrum lībertī et medicī Augustī saepius
ventitāvērunt quam ex mōre prīncipum. incertum est utrum vēnerint ut
eum cūrārent an ut morbī causās cognōscerent. dīcunt nōnnūllī scrīptōrēs
mōmenta ipsa Agricolae morientis Domitiānō nūntiāta esse per cursōrēs
dispositōs. Domitiānus ipse, īrā satiātā, sē maximō dolōre affectum esse   *10*
simulāvit.

    satis cōnstat Agricolam in testāmentō Domitiānum fēcisse cohērēdem
optimae uxōrī et piissimae fīliae; quō cognitō Domitiānum esse laetātum.
mēns eius tam caeca et adulātiōne corrupta erat ut nescīret nūllum
prīncipem hērēdem fierī nisi malum.   *15*

suīs: suī	*his family*
lūctuōsus	*sorrowful*
bonīs: bonī	*decent citizens*
circulōs: circulus	*club*
quisquam	*anyone*
laetātus est: laetārī	*be glad*
ventitāvērunt: ventitāre	*keep coming*
ex mōre	*according to the custom*
mōmenta: mōmentum	*critical stage*
cursōrēs dispositōs:	
cursor dispositus	*relay runner*
satiātā: satiātus	*satiated, appeased*
cohērēdem: cohērēs	*joint heir*
piissimae: pius	*devoted, loving*

1 Who were affected by Agricola's death?
2 Where in Rome was his death discussed?
3 What is the contrast implied by the two phrases: **per fora, per circulōs**
    (line 3)?
4 Does Tacitus state that Agricola was poisoned or merely imply it? If
    you think Tacitus is not sure whether Agricola was poisoned, why
    then do you think he mentions poison at all?
5 What are the two possible reasons that Tacitus states for the emperor's
    sending freedmen and doctors from the palace? Which of the two do
    you think Tacitus believes? Why?

6 Do we have proof or simply Tacitus' assertion that Domitian *pretended* to be sorry? Could Tacitus have known for sure?
7 Why do you think Agricola would have made Domitian co-heir in his will?
8 What does **satis cōnstat** (line 12) mean? Why do you think Tacitus uses the phrase here?

37.5 Word Power

Match the definition to the English derivative.

1 elation
2 initiation
3 perturbation
4 validation
5 auriferous
6 invidious
7 odious

a gold-bearing
b a disturbance
c disgusting, offensive
d a feeling of pride or happiness
e exciting envy or ill will
f proof; confirmation
g an introduction

37.6 The Emperor's Council

Read pages 53–54 in your textbook and answer the following:

1 Give the Latin expression for the people who helped the emperor in the government of the empire. To what group did they belong?
2 How did one become a member of the emperor's special group?
3 List two types of members of this group.
4 What happened to the group when the emperor changed?
5 List four types of matters for which the emperor might seek advice from this group.
6 What was the most frequent task of group members?
7 Describe specifically how the emperor consulted these members.
8 In theory how should members have responded? What happened under certain emperors? How did some members behave during Domitian's reign?
9 Describe two matters Pliny referred to Emperor Trajan for advice.
10 Why was this group a necessity for the emperor?

The Senatorial Career – cursus honōrum

The steps in the senatorial career were carefully marked out by tradition, as well as the normal ages at which the highest positions were usually held. Many persons would not have climbed all the steps.

Study pages 54–56 in your textbook, and then describe the duties associated with each position in the space provided.

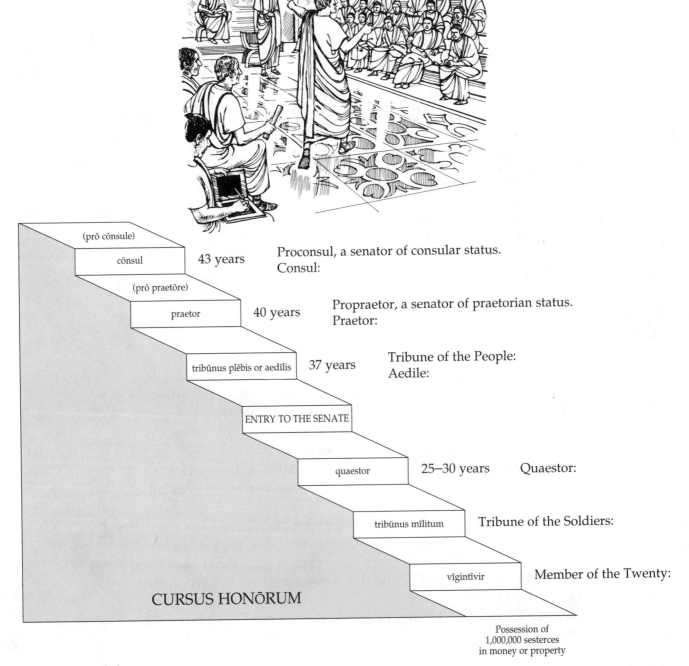

(prō cōnsule)

cōnsul   43 years

Proconsul, a senator of consular status.
Consul:

(prō praetōre)

praetor   40 years

Propraetor, a senator of praetorian status.
Praetor:

tribūnus plēbis or aedīlis   37 years

Tribune of the People:
Aedile:

ENTRY TO THE SENATE

quaestor   25–30 years   Quaestor:

tribūnus mīlitum   Tribune of the Soldiers:

vīgintīvir   Member of the Twenty:

CURSUS HONŌRUM

Possession of
1,000,000 sesterces
in money or property

Pliny and Cicero write to their wives.

Translate the following two letters. Then answer the questions that follow.

A PLINY TO CALPURNIA:
scrībis tē absentiā meā nōn mediocriter adficī, ūnumque habēre
solācium, quod prō mē libellōs meōs teneās et saepe in vestīgiō meō
collocēs. grātum est quod nōs requīris, grātum quod hīs fōmentīs
adquiēscis. invicem ego epistulās tuās lectitō atque identidem in
manūs quasi novās sūmō. sed eō magis ad dēsīderium tuī accendor!   5
tū tamen quam frequentissimē scrībe, quamquam hoc ita mē dēlectat
ut torqueat. valē.

mediocriter	*a little*	fōmentīs:	
adficī: adficere	*affect*	fōmentum	*consolation*
quod	*that, the fact that*	adquiēscis:	
		adquiēscere	*find comfort*
prō	*in place of, instead of*	lectitō: lectitāre	*read and re-read*
		sūmō: sūmere	*take, pick up*
vestīgiō: vestīgium	*place*	eō magis	*all the more*
collocēs: collocāre	*place, set, put*	dēsīderium:	
grātum: grātus	*pleasing*	dēsīderium	*longing*
requīris: requīrere	*miss, need, long for*	accendor:	
		accendere	*set on fire*

B CICERO TO TERENTIA:
in Tusculānum nōs ventūrōs putāmus aut Nōnīs aut postrīdiē. ibi, ut
sint omnia parāta (plūrēs enim fortasse nōbīscum erunt, et, ut arbitror,
diūtius ibi commorābimur). labrum sī in balineō nōn est, ut sit, item
cētera quae sunt ad victum et ad valētūdinem necessāria. valē.

Tusculānum:	*our Tusculan villa*	commorābimur:	
Tusculānus	*(one of Cicero's country estates)*	commorārī	*stay, remain*
		labrum	*basin,*
ventūrōs = ventūrōs esse			*wash-basin*
Nōnīs	*on the Nones*	balineō:	
ut sint = fac ut sint; cūrā ut sint		balineum	*bath, bathroom*
plūrēs	*several (men)*	item	*likewise*
arbitror:		victum: victus	*good living*
arbitrārī	*think, believe*	valētūdinem:	
diūtius	*for some time*	valētūdō	*good health*

1 What gives Calpurnia consolation? What gives Pliny consolation?
2 If you were Calpurnia, how would you feel on receiving Pliny's letter?
3 If you were Terentia, how would you feel on receiving Cicero's letter?
4 What features in Cicero's letter might especially annoy Terentia?

25

Find the Latin idiom.

A *Unscramble the words on the left, and then fill in the squares. The circled letters will spell a Latin idiom common in the Unit 4 textbook. The English translations are given as hints in parentheses.*

	Hints
EPATO	(poet)
MESCO	(comrade)
SHEMI	(winter)
NENNO	(surely...?)
ALIFI	(daughter)
SAFUR	(trick)
DUALO	(I praise)
ARUQE	(why?)
ROPIR	(in front, earlier)
IMATE	(even, also)

B *Read the letters in the squares with circles. What is the Latin idiom? What does it mean?*

Tenses of the Subjunctive

Translate the following sentences into English:

1 quis scit cūr amīcī hoc dōnum ēmerint?
2 in animō volvunt num Agricola revocētur.
3 māter rogāvit quis fīliam vexāret.
4 nūntāvistīne quandō hūc missus essēs?
5 vōbīs explicandum est quid factum sit.
6 centuriō nesciēbat quō mīlitēs fūgissent.
7 nunc cognōscō quō modō barbarī vīvant.
8 dīxitne quī servī pūnīrentur?

Sparsus says to Polla that …

In the indirect statements below, choose the correct Latin word in each set of parentheses and then translate the entire indirect sentence.

1   "pontifex iam porcum sacrificāvit."
    INDIRECT: Sparsus Pōllae dīcit (pontificem/pontifex) iam porcum
         (sacrificāre/sacrificāvisse).

2   "pontifex deīs precēs offert."
    INDIRECT ACTIVE: Sparsus Pōllae dīcit (pontificem/pontifex) deīs precēs
         (offerre/obtulisse).

3   "precēs deīs ā pontifice offeruntur."
    INDIRECT PASSIVE: Sparsus Pōllae dīcit precēs deīs
         (ā pontifice/pontifex) (offerrī/oblātōs esse).

4   "ego et tū nūptiās mox celebrābimus."
    INDIRECT: Sparsus Pōllae dīcit sē et Pōllam nūptiās mox
         (celebrātūrōs esse/celebrāre).

5   "ego et tū posteā ad triclīnium prōcēdēmus et cēnam cōnsūmēmus."
    INDIRECT: Sparsus Pōllae dīcit sē et Pōllam posteā ad triclīnium
         (prōcessūrōs esse/prōcessisse) et cēnam
         (cōnsūmptūrōs esse/cōnsūmere).

27

38.5 Wedding Song

The following stanzas are taken from a poem by Catullus, written for the wedding of Junia and Manlius. The poem starts with an invocation (a formal prayer to a god or goddess to be present) to Hymen, the god of marriage.

In the right-hand column, fill in the relevant information from the poem.

Invocation and description of Hymen, sung on the way to the bride's house

1 collis ō Helicōniī
cultor, Ūraniae genus,
quī rapis teneram ad virum
virginem, ō Hymenaee Hymēn,
    ō Hymēn Hymenaee

Where Hymen lives and what he does

_____
_____

2 cinge tempora flōribus
suāve olentis amāracī,
flammeum cape, laetus hūc
hūc venī niveō gerēns
    lūteum pede soccum,

Appearance of Hymen

_____
_____

3 excitusque hilarī diē,
nūptiālia concinēns
vōce carmina tinnulā,
pelle humum pedibus, manū
    pīneam quate taedam.

What Hymen needs to do

_____
_____

Reason for the song

4 namque Iūnia Manliō,
quālis Īdalium colēns
venit ad Phrygium Venus
iūdicem, bona cum bonā
    nūbet ālite virgō.

a Prediction for Junia and Manlius
_____

b Simile for Junia and Manlius
_____

5 ac domum dominam vocā
coniugis cupidam novī,
mentem amōre revinciēns,
ut tenax edera hūc et hūc
    arborem implicat errāns.

a More instructions for Hymen
_____

b Another simile for the bride
_____

Guests at the bride's house

6 claustra pandite iānuae,
virgō adest. vidēn ut facēs
splendidās quatiunt comās?
[break in the MS]

Events at the bride's house
_____
_____

28

7 tālis in variō solet
   dīvitis dominī hortulō
   stāre flōs hyacinthus
   sed morāris, abit diēs,
      prōdeās, nova nūpta.

a Simile for the bride

   _____

b Instructions to the bride

   _____

On the way to the groom's house

8 tollite, ō puerī, facēs:
   flammeum videō venīre.
   īte, concinite in modum
   "iō Hymēn Hymenaee iō,
      iō Hymēn Hymenaee."

Features of the bridal procession

   _____

   _____

At the groom's house

9 trānsfer ōmine cum bonō
   līmen aureolōs pedēs,
   rāsilemque subī forem.
   iō Hymēn Hymenaee iō,
      iō Hymēn Hymenaee.

Instructions to the bride arriving at the groom's house

   _____

   _____

collis: collis	*hill*	colēns: colere	*inhabit, protect*
Helicōniī: Helicōnius	*of Helicon* (hill of the Muses)	Phrygium: Phrygius	*Phrygian, Trojan* (Paris)
cultor: cultor	*protector, inhabitant*	ālite: āles	*omen, bird*
Ūraniae: Ūrania	*Urania* (a Muse)	revinciēns: revincīre	*tie, fasten*
genus: genus	*child*	tenax	*clinging*
cinge: cingere	*wreathe*	edera	*ivy*
tempora: tempus	*forehead, temple*	implicat: implicāre	*enfold, entwine*
suāve	*sweetly*	claustra: claustra	*bars, bolts*
olentis: olēre	*smell*	pandite: pandere	*open*
amāracī: amāracus	*marjoram plant*	vidēn = vidēsne	
niveō: niveus	*snow-white*	ut	*how*
lūteum: lūteus	*yellow*	comās: coma	*hair*
soccum: soccus	*shoe*	variō: varius	*many-colored*
excitus: excīre	*rouse*	hortulō: hortulus	*little garden*
hilarī: hilaris	*happy, high-spirited*	prōdeās: prōdīre	*come out*
concinēns: concinere	*sing*	in modum	*in rhythm*
tinnula: tinnulus	*ringing*	trānsfer … pedēs	*step over* (take the feet across)
pelle: pellere	*strike*		
pīneam: pīneus	*pinewood*		
quate: quatere	*shake*	aureolōs: aureolus	*gold-colored*
taedam: taeda	*torch*	rāsilem: rāsilis	*polished*
Īdalium: Īdalium	*Idalium* (town in Cyprus, sacred to Venus)	subī: subīre	*go inside*
		forem: foris	*door, entrance*

29

Word Power

A *The word **vestis** yields a number of derivatives, some of which have lost most of their connection with clothing. Match them to these definitions:*

1 a room in a church for ceremonial robes
2 an installing in office with ceremony
3 to lay out capital with a view to profit
4 burlesque imitation of a work
5 a facing of a wall with brick or stone
6 that which cannot be taken away, as in interest

a investiture
b travesty
c revetment
d vested
e vestry
f invest

B *Fill in the blanks with derivatives from words on the Stage 38 Vocabulary Checklist, using the underlined English to assist you:*

1 The _____ profession is concerned with the <u>law</u>.

2 Technically speaking, if you _____ someone, you could be said to throw that person <u>out of the threshold</u>.

3 He took an _____ test, to see if his field of employment was <u>suitable</u>.

4 _____ sports take place <u>inside</u> a school's <u>walls</u>.

5 The _____ mood of the verb usually indicates that it is in a part of the sentence <u>joined under</u> the main part.

6 The _____ will be solemnized this afternoon as Marcus and Maria are joined in <u>marriage</u>.

38.7 Marriage

Read pages 75–78 in your textbook and answer the following:

1 What was the average age for a Roman girl to marry? A Roman man?
2 How was the husband selected? What had to happen by law before the marriage could take place?
3 What was the **dōs**?
4 Describe five aspects of a Roman **spōnsālia**.
5 Outline three aspects of marriage **cum manū**.
6 How did the ceremony of **cōnfarreātiō** get its name?
7 Outline four aspects of marriage **sine manū**.
8 Explain the following terms as they relate to a Roman wedding:
   a **bulla**   e **iūnctiō dextrārum**
   b **larēs**   f **cēna nūptiālis**
   c **flammeum**   g **ubi tū Gāius, ego Gāia**
   d **haruspex**   h **mātrōnae ūnivirae**
9 List nine other customs of a Roman wedding.
10 What was the chief purpose of a Roman marriage? List two ways Emperor Augustus encouraged marriage and large families. How successful was he?
11 What were five things a Roman wife couldn't do? What were four things that she could?
12 What was a Roman wife's traditional role? Why was that role considered demanding?
13 Why is our view of Roman married life very incomplete?
14 What are two types of sources for what we do know about married life?

Quīntiliānus dē discipulīs

*Quintilian, the rhetor assigned to teach Domitian's adopted sons, wrote a treatise on educating young boys (*Institutio Oratoria*). Read through these passages on his idea of an ideal student, and answer the questions which follow.*

A

ingeniī signum in parvīs praecipuum memoria est: eius duplex virtūs, facile percipere et fidēliter continēre.

praecipuum: praecipuus	*special, excellent*
duplex	*double, two-fold*
percipere	*understand, grasp*
continēre	*retain*

1 What does Quintilian consider an excellent indicator of intelligence in small children?
2 What two virtues does this indicator have?

B

probus quoque in prīmīs erit ille vērē ingeniōsus. aliōquī nōn peius dūxerim tardī esse ingenī quam malī.

probus (= probus puer)	*good, virtuous*
vērē ingeniōsus	*truly intelligent, truly talented*
aliōquī	*otherwise*
nōn peius dūxerim	*I would not consider worse*
ingenī = ingeniī	

1 What two qualities does Quintilian consider inseparable?
2 What two types of student does Quintilian mention in the second sentence? How does he compare them?

C

hic meus (puer) nōn difficulter accipiet, quaedam etiam interrogābit. sequētur tamen magis quam praecurret. illud ingeniōrum praecox genus nōn temere umquam pervenit ad frūgem.

accipiet: accipere	*learn*
praecurret: praecurrere	*run ahead*
praecox: praecox	*precocious*
nōn temere	*not easily, not often*
frūgem: frux	*fruition, success*

1 How would Quintilian's ideal student learn? How should he not behave?
2 What is Quintilian's opinion of precocious children?

D

mihi ille dētur puer quem laus excitet, quem glōria iuvet, quī victus fleat.
hic erit alendus ambitū, hunc mordēbit obiurgātiō, hunc honor excitābit,
in hōc dēsidiam numquam verēbor.

mihi … dētur puer	*let me be given a boy*	ambitū: ambitus	*ambition*
laus	*praise*	mordēbit: mordēre	*bite, sting*
fleat: flēre	*weep*	obiurgātiō	*criticism, blame*
alendus: alere	*feed, nourish*	dēsidiam: dēsidia	*apathy, idleness*

1 Give three qualities Quintilian would like to see in a student.
2 What four effects would those qualities have?

Do you agree or disagree with Quintilian's opinions?
How would you rate as a student in his eyes?

39.2 Change a letter and change the meaning.

*On a separate piece of paper, translate each sentence below. Then change the
underlined letter in each sentence so that the new word matches the English
translation in parentheses, and retranslate the new sentence. (Ignore the position
of the long marks.)*

1 nōlī deās culpāre.   (gods)
2 puer dentem āmīsit.   (mind)
3 puella mātrem amat.   (father)
4 hic est agnus Deī.   (year)
5 pater fīlium dūcit.   (daughter)
6 fēminae rēgēs laudant.   (laws)
7 cinis dēcidit.   (citizen)
8 puerī lūdōs amant.   (wolves)
9 morsus canis gravis est. (illness)

39.3 Word Power: Same Difference

*Complete the following analogies with a word from the Stage 39 Vocabulary
Checklist:*

1 et : ac :: igitur : ____
2 ēgredī : exīre :: dēlēre : ____
3 morior : mortem obeō :: dēcipiō : ____
4 at : sed :: vel : ____
5 dīves : pauper :: orior : ____

He says that ...

Fill in each blank with the correct form of the Latin word which translates the underlined word(s) in the English translation.

1 "mī Quīnte," inquit Cogidubnus, "tū mihi cōnsilium optimum dās."

Cogidubnus dīcit _____ sibi

cōnsilium optimum _____.

Cogidubnus says that <u>Quintus is giving</u> him the best advice.

2 "domine, domine," inquit Cephalus, "Gāius Salvius thermīs appropinquat."

Cephalus dominō dīcit _____.

_____ thermīs _____.

Cephalus says to his master that <u>Gaius Salvius is approaching</u> the baths.

3 "Quīntus Caecilius," inquit Rūfus, "epistulam portat."

Rūfus dīcit _____ _____

epistulam _____.

Rufus says that <u>Quintus Caecilius is carrying</u> a letter.

34

4 "Agricola," inquit Salvius, "tū in Calēdoniā bellum geris et victōriās inānēs refers."

Salvius dīcit Agricolam in

Calēdoniā bellum _____

et victōriās inānēs _____ .

Salvius says that Agricola <u>is waging</u> war in Caledonia and <u>is bringing back</u> meaningless victories.

5 "Rōmānī," inquit pāstor, "casam meam incendunt."

pāstor dīcit _____ casam

suam _____ .

The shepherd says that <u>the Romans are burning</u> his house.

39.5 Instructive Gerundives

Working in pairs, take turns to give each other instructions according to the gerundive phrases below, e.g. **cōnsīde pictūrae pingendae causā**. *(Sit down to paint a picture.) The student receiving the instructions carries them out in silence.*

surge/cōnsīde

   cantandī carminis causā
   ad librum legendum
   pictūrae pingendae causā
   ad sellam tollendam
   stilī dēponendī causā
   ad fābulam agendam
   discipulī spectandī causā
   ad fenestram aperiendam
   mūrī tangendī causā

Domitian's Total Change of Character

Read the following passage, based on Suetonius' Life of Domitian. Then answer the questions below.

cupiditātis atque avāritiae suspīciōnem
nūllam aut prīvātus umquam aut
prīnceps diū dedit. pecūniam sibi
relictam ab eīs, quibus līberī erant, nōn
accēpit. accūsātiōnēs falsās magnā   5
dēlātōrum poenā repressit. "prīnceps,"
inquit Domitiānus, "quī dēlātōrēs nōn
castīgat, incitat."

neque in clēmentiā neque in
abstinentiā mānsit, sed saevus factus est   10
celerius quam avārus. discipulum
Paridis pantomīmī puerum adhūc et
praetereā aegerrimum, quod arte
fōrmāque nōn dissimilis magistrō Paridī
vidēbātur, occīdit. Helvidiumque   15
Prīscum occīdit, quasi in fābulā dē Paride et Oenōnē compositā dīvortium
suum ab uxōre Domitiā reprehendisset. et occīdit Flāvium Sabīnum
patruēlem, quod comitiōrum cōnsulārium diē praecō ad populum eum
nōn cōnsulem dēsignātum prōnūntiāverat sed imperātōrem.

cupiditātis: cupiditās	*greed* (for money)
avāritiae: avāritia	*avarice, stinginess*
dēlātōrum: dēlātor	*informer, dishonest spy*
repressit: reprimere	*repress, put a stop to*
neque = nec	
clēmentiā: clēmentia	*leniency, mercy*
abstinentiā: abstinentia	*self-control*
quasi	*on the assumption that*
dīvortium: dīvortium	*divorce*
patruēlem: patruēlis	*cousin* (descended from his father's brother)
comitiōrum cōnsulārium:	
comitia cōnsulāria	*elections for the consuls*
cōnsulem dēsignātum:	
cōnsul dēsignātus	*consul elect*

1 Which traits of character did Domitian *not* exhibit at first? How did he
   show generosity at first?
2 When Domitian changed for the worse, which trait of character
   became dominant?

3 Why did Domitian have the apprentice-dancer executed? Why, according to Suetonius, was the execution of this dancer especially cruel?

4 Why did Domitian have the writer Helvidius Priscus the Younger executed?

5 Research the myth of Paris and Oenone in a handbook of classical mythology. Which episode of the myth of Paris and Oenone paralleled Domitian's real life? Why might Domitian have objected to being apparently compared to the mythical Paris?

6 Do you think the herald's mistake (confusing consul with emperor) might have been an easy one? Why?

39.7 Fearful Mix-up

Working in a group and using a separate piece of paper, Student A writes a word from each of columns 1 and 2, and then folds the paper over so that no word is visible. A passes the paper to B, who writes ut or nē below the fold, folds that over, and passes the paper to C. C writes a word from column 4, and folds that over before passing it to D. D writes a phrase from column 5, folds the paper and passes it to E. E writes a word or phrase from the last column and then unfolds the paper. The whole group then reads and translates the given sentence.

e.g. socius verētur nē exercitus in proeliō vincātur.
The ally fears that the army may be conquered in battle.

lēgātus	verētur	ut/nē	praefectus	cum hostibus	rīdeat
coniūnx			vicīnus	in cūriā	mentiātur
magistrātus			cōnsul	in forō	vestēs āmittat
discipulus			senātor	in agrō	querātur
socius			exercitus	in proeliō	vincātur
māter			senex	in līmine	sedeat
medicus			vespillō	in cloācā	medicīnam cōnsūmat
amīcus			rhētor	in carcere	discipulum retineat

Authors, Readers, and Listeners

Read pages 96–98 in your textbook and answer the following:

1 If an author decided to make his work available to the general public, how might **librāriī** and **bibliopōlae** help him?
2 Where would one go in Rome to buy books? How much would a small ordinary book cost? A deluxe edition?
3 Who made money on the book sales?
4 By what two means could an author support himself?
5 Why would one want to be a **patrōnus** for an author?
6 Tell how the Emperor Augustus was involved in the works of Vergil and Horace.
7 In what two ways did Ovid displease the Emperor Augustus? What did Augustus do to Ovid as a result?
8 To what extent did Martial's works meet the approval of Emperor Domitian?
9 What type of literature reached a wide public? For what type of audience did most Roman authors write?
10 Who was the first teacher to receive a salary from the state? What was his most influential book? What did it cover?
11 Explain how the study of rhetoric influenced the way Latin literature was written.
12 What is the most important difference between Latin and modern literature?
13 Explain how this difference between Latin and modern literature affected the way Roman authors wrote.
14 Explain how written Latin literature is compared to a page of music.

40.1 Pliny prosecutes in a senate trial.

In the following letter, Pliny describes his experiences in a Senate trial of A.D. 100. Pliny, instructed to act on behalf of the people of the province of Africa, spoke for the prosecution against Marius Priscus, an ex-governor of that province. One of the speakers for the defense will be familiar to you. Emperor Trajan presided.

Read the passage and answer the questions that follow.

A clepsydra.

in senātū augustissimō praesente Imperātōre mihi dīcendum erat.
imāgināre mihi metum! cum tamen animum cōgitātiōnemque
collēgissem, dīcere coepī. dīxī hōrās paene quīnque; nam duodecim
clepsydrīs spatiōsissimīs, quās accēperam, sunt additae quattuor.
Imperātor quidem tantum mihi studium, tantam etiam cūram (nimium   5
est enim dīcere sollicitūdinem) praestitit, ut lībertum meum post mē
stantem saepius admonēret ut vōcī et laterī cōnsulerem.
    postrīdiē dīxit prō Priscō Salvius Līberālis, vir subtīlis, dispositus,
ācer, disertus; in illā vērō causā omnēs artēs suās prōtulit.

augustissimō: augustus	*majestic, dignified*
imāgināre	*imagine* (imperative of **imāginārī**)
cōgitātiōnem: cōgitātiō	*thought*
clepsydrīs: clepsydra	*water-clock*
spatiōsissimīs: spatiōsus	*large, ample*
sollicitūdinem: sollicitūdō	*anxiety*
laterī: latus	*side, lungs*
cōnsulerem: cōnsulere	*be concerned about*
subtīlis	*discriminating, precise*
dispositus	*orderly, methodical*
ācer	*sharp, forceful*
disertus	*fluent*
prōtulit: prōferre	*bring forward*

39

1 Suggest two reasons why Pliny was nervous (line 1).
2 How many measures of the water-clock were originally assigned to Pliny? Who would have granted extra time?
3 The emperor spoke to Pliny indirectly, through his freedman. Why would Pliny have had a freedman standing behind him? If the emperor was concerned about Pliny's voice and lungs, what can you infer about Pliny's speaking style?
4 Pliny describes Salvius as **subtīlis**, **dispositus**, **ācer**, **disertus**. What is the effect of clustering these adjectives without **et** or **-que**?
5 Recalling other stories involving Salvius, describe episodes which support or contradict Pliny's description.

40.2 A Vestal Virgin is buried alive.

The Vestal Virgins were six priestesses charged with watching the eternal fire of the Roman hearth-goddess, Vesta. The Temple of Vesta was in the Forum. Vestal Virgins, as their name implies, were expected to be chaste.

The Emperor Domitian invoked an ancient, but rarely used law to condemn a Vestal Virgin named Cornelia to death by burial while still alive. It is not clear whether she was guilty or not.

Read the following excerpt based on a letter by Pliny. Then answer the questions.

Domitian decided to bury alive Cornelia (the high priestess of the Vestal Virgins), intending to make his reign memorable with a moral example of this kind. Acting on his authority as **pontifex maximus** he summoned the other priests to meet at his palace on the banks of Lake Albanus (about 15 miles from Rome) instead of in Rome on the Palatine Hill, and there he condemned Cornelia without allowing her to appear in person or defend herself.

40

pontificēs ad Cornēliam dēfodiendam necandamque statim Romam missī sunt. quae nunc ad Vestam, nunc ad cēterōs deōs manūs extendēns frequentissimē clāmābat: "mē Imperātor incestam putat, sed cum sacrificia facerem, ille et vīcit et triumphāvit." dubium est utrum hoc ex fidūciā an ex contemptū Imperātōris dīxerit.   5

nescio an innocēns fuerit, sed certē tamquam innocēns mortua est; nam stola, cum carnifex Cornēliam in subterrāneum specum dēmitteret, saxō haesit, et cum carnifex eī manum daret, resiluit et foedum contāctum quasi plānē ā castō pūrōque corpore reiēcit.

dēfodiendam: dēfodere	*bury in the earth*
incestam: incestus	*unchaste, lewd*
fidūciā: fidūcia	*self-confidence*
subterrāneum: subterrāneus	*underground*
specum: specus	*cave, chamber*
resiluit: resilīre	*jump back*
plānē	*clearly, obviously*
castō: castus	*chaste*

1 Why do you think the emperor called together the other priests at a location outside Rome to discuss Cornelia's fate?
2 Cornelia reminded the emperor that he had been militarily successful when she had made sacrifices to the gods for him. What reasons does Pliny suggest for her saying this? What do *you* think?
3 Why do you think Cornelia refused help (with freeing her dress) from the executioner?
4 Does Pliny provide clear proof for any of your answers to the questions above? Or does he simply suggest possibilities? Explain.

40.3 Indirect Questions and Direct Answers

In each question-and-answer pair below, choose the correct Latin word, and then translate the completed sentences.

1 scīsne quot basilicae in hāc pictūrā (sunt/sint)? sunt partēs (duārum/trium) basilicārum.

2 scīsne ā quibus causae in hīs basilicīs (aguntur/agantur)? causae ab (ōrātōribus/uxōribus) in hīs basilicīs aguntur.

3 scīsne cuius templum (stet/stat) iuxtā basilicam Iūliam? templum (Concordiae/Saturnī) iuxtā basilicam Iūliam stat.

4 scīsne ubi Rōstra in forō (sunt/sint)? Rōstra inter basilicās (sint/sunt).

5 scīsne quae in Rōstrīs (fīant/fīunt)? ōrātiōnēs in Rōstrīs (habentur/habeantur).

6 scīsne in quō monte templum Iovis Optimī et Maximī (stat/stet)? templum Iovis Optimī et Maximī in monte (Palātīnō/Capitōlīnō) (stet/stat).

Audīte/Dīcite

*Fold the page in half so that each partner sees only one column. **A** begins by asking a question. **B** responds, making the correct choice from two alternatives. **A** verifies this choice. Then **B** asks a question, and the process continues.*

A	**B**
1 quārē sociōs prōdidistī? (pecūniae accipiendae causā hoc fēcī.)	1 pecūniae accipiendae causā hoc fēcī. dīligenter labōrandō hoc fēcī.
2 ad cūriam intrandam vēnī. nāvigandō vēnī.	2 quō modō hūc vēnistī? (nāvigandō vēnī.)
3 quid dē rhētore exīstimās? (est perītus dīcendī.)	3 ad Caesarem laudandum vēnistī. est perītus dīcendī.
4 ad tumultum effugiendum currēbam. cupidī currendī sunt.	4 cūr per viam currēbās? (ad tumultum effugiendum currēbam.)
5 quid Imperātōrī respondistī? (eum moderātiōne suādendō lēnīvī.)	5 parātus est ad crīmen explicandum. eum moderātiōne suādendō lēnīvī.
6 vīnum amphorīs īnferendīs effūdī. vīnum ad bibendum effūdī.	6 quārē vīnum effūdistī? (vīnum ad bibendum effūdī.)
7 cūr tam miser es? (nūllam occāsiōnem habeō innocentiae probandae.)	7 nūllam occāsiōnem habeō innocentiae probandae. docendō discimus.
8 vulnere fingendō proelium vītāvī. proeliō vītandō tūtus manēbam.	8 quō modō proelium vītāvistī? (vulnere fingendō proelium vītāvī.)
9 quō modō domum servāvistī? (flammīs exstinguendīs domum servāvī.)	9 dominī iuvandī causā domum servāvī. flammīs exstinguendīs domum servāvī.
10 ad iuvandum festīnāvī. in librīs legendīs occupātī sunt.	10 quid dē incendiō fēcistī? (ad iuvandum festīnāvī.)

40.5 Marcus Metellus Fortūnātus

A *Fill the blanks in both parts of the story below (about an old-time con man) with the appropriate infinitive from the box.*

1 | amāre esse velle vēnisse nātum esse
vīsitātūrum esse   datūrum esse

ōlim homō quīdam ad parvum oppidum pervēnit. nūntiāvit sē M.
Metellum Fortūnātum _____; sē nōbilissimā gente _____; sē
ab urbe Rōmā _____. quō audītō, omnēs magistrātūs et cēterī
dīvitēs inter sē certābant ut eum domōs suās invītārent. ille
prōmīsit sē omnēs _____. itaque multōs diēs grātīs et magnificē   5
cēnābat.

   dum in hōc oppidō manet, saepe ad forum ambulābat. ibi
multīs rēbus pretiōsīs ā mercātōribus comparātīs, sē pecūniam mox
_____ affirmābat.

   deinde viduam dīvitissimam colere coepit, quae amōre incēnsa   10
multa dōna eī dedit. Metellus simulāvit sē quoque eam valdē
_____ et in mātrimōnium dūcere _____.

   cum tamen diēs nūptiārum vēnisset, Metellus āfuit; neque ā
cīvibus umquam posteā vīsus est.

grātīs *for free*   viduam: vidua *widow*   colere *woo, court*

2 | recubuisse exclāmāvisse respondisse habuisse
cēnāvisse ēiectum esse profectum esse

paucīs post mēnsibus mercātor quīdam cum ad hoc oppidum
pervēnisset in tabernam intrāvit, ubi colloquium dē sceleribus
Metellī habēbātur.

   "hunc hominem cognōvī!" exclāmāvit mercātor. "vultisne scīre
quid eī acciderit?"   5

   tum omnibus rogantibus dīxit Metellum, postquam ex oppidō
discessisset, Rōmam _____; ibi saepe apud multōs dīvitēs
_____; deinde cum ad cēnam splendidam invītātus esset, prope

44

senātōrem splendidam togam gerentem _____ ; cum eō

colloquium _____ ; ubi senātōr nōmen rogāvisset, eum _____ *10*

sē M. Metellum Fortūnātum esse; quō audītō, alterum īrātum

_____ ,

"longē errās, sceleste! ego ipse sum M. Metellus Fortūnātus.

servī, hunc hominem verberāte."

quō factō, eum domō ā servīs _____ . *15*

B *Translate the completed story.*

Quintus says/said that …

In the indirect statements below, choose the
correct Latin word in each set of parentheses, and
then translate the entire indirect sentence.

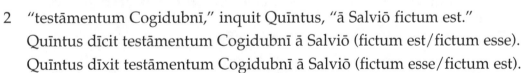

1 DIRECT: "Salvius," inquit Quīntus, "mortem rēgī Cogidubnō parāvit."

 INDIRECT: Quīntus dīcit (Salvium/Salvius) mortem rēgī Cogidubnō (parāvit/parāvisse).

 INDIRECT: Quīntus dīxit (Salvium/Salvius) mortem rēgī Cogidubnō (parāvisse/parāvit).

2 "testāmentum Cogidubnī," inquit Quīntus, "ā Salviō fictum est."

 Quīntus dīcit testāmentum Cogidubnī ā Salviō (fictum est/fictum esse).

 Quīntus dīxit testāmentum Cogidubnī ā Salviō (fictum esse/fictum est).

3 "Salvius," inquit Quīntus, "duōs tripodas argenteōs, ā mē Cogidubnō datōs, domī habet."

 Quīntus dīcit (Salvius/Salvium) duōs tripodas argenteōs, ā sē Cogidubnō datōs, domī (habet/habēre).

 Quīntus dīxit (Salvium/Salviō) duōs tripodas argenteōs, ā sē Cogidubnō datōs, domī (habēre/habuisse).

4 "Salvius," inquit Quīntus, "poenam dabit."

 Quīntus dīcit (Salvium/Salvius) poenam (datūrum esse/dabit).

 Quīntus dīxit (Salviī/Salvium) poenam (dare/datūrum esse).

45

40.7 Word Power: A Ten-tion

Give a definition for each of the underlined words below:

1 affirmation of the president's decision
2 receiving the approbation of the crowd
3 the assimilation of minorities into society
4 guilt by association
5 the commutation of the sentence by the judge
6 the configuration of the planets
7 a suit for defamation of character
8 the levitation of a subject by the magician
9 an objection to the new policy
10 transcendental meditation

40.8 Roman Law Courts

Read pages 115–118 in your textbook and answer the following:

1 Explain what happened in the following cases during the first century A.D.:
   a   criminal offenses   b   civil cases
2 With what type of civil cases did the **centumvirī** deal?
3 Describe what could happen to senators charged with crimes during Domitian's time.
4 Explain the three main differences between Roman and modern times in handling criminal charges.
5 List three ways success as a speaker in court could affect a Roman citizen.
6 What were the expected rewards for the people who conducted court cases?
7 Explain the difference between Roman courts in the first century B.C. and during the time of Domitian.
8 Which three authors gave vivid details about the liveliness and excitement in courts? List seven details they mentioned.
9 Indicate two tactics used in Roman courts to sway the jury.
10 While it is difficult to judge the overall fairness of Roman courts, what do the writings of Pliny and Quintilian show?
11 How did the following terms affect the fairness of Roman courts: **lēgēs, decemvirī lēgibus scrībendīs,** and **duodecim tabulae**?
12 How could one describe Roman law at its best? For what did Roman law become the basis?

What shall we do about the Christians?

One of the most famous exchanges of letters between Pliny and Trajan concerned Pliny's dealings with the Christians. Organizations of all kinds had been banned in Bithynia because of unrest. In addition, refusing to take the oath of allegiance to the emperor (which involved worshiping the Roman gods) was treason. In the excerpts printed below, Pliny explains how he has handled the situation so far, and Trajan replies with some general rules for handling evidence and punishment.
   Translate into English.

C. Plīnius Trāiānō Imperātōrī

sollemne est mihi, domine, omnia dē quibus dubitō ad tē referre. quis enim potest melius cunctātiōnem meam regere vel ignōrantiam īnstruere? cognitiōnibus dē Christiānīs interfuī numquam; ideō nescio quid pūnīrī soleat.   5

   interim, iīs quī tamquam Christiānī ad mē dēferēbantur hunc sum secūtus modum. interrogāvī ipsōs an essent Christiānī. cōnfitentēs iterum ac tertiō interrogāvī, supplicium minātus; persevērantēs dūcī iussī. neque enim dubitābam pertināciam et īnflexibilem obstinātiōnem dēbēre pūnīrī. fuērunt aliī similis āmentiae, quōs, quia cīvēs Rōmānī erant,   10 adnotāvī in Urbem remittendōs.

   prōpositus est libellus sine auctōre multōrum nōmina continēns. quī negābant esse sē Christiānōs aut fuisse, cum, praeeunte mē, deōs appellārent et imāginī tuae tūre ac vīnō supplicārent dīmittendōs esse putāvī.   15

sollemne: sollemnis	*customary, normal*	āmentiae: āmentia	*folly, fanaticism*
cunctātiōnem: cunctātiō	*hesitancy*	adnotāvī: adnotāre	*note, write down*
regere	*resolve, deal with*		
īnstruere	*instruct, direct*	prōpositus est:	*present, put forward*
cognitiōnibus: cognitiō	*trial*	prōpōnere	
interfuī: interesse	*be present at, attend*	libellus sine auctōre	*an anonymous pamphlet*
ideō	*and so, for that reason*	quī = eōs quī	
		negābant: negāre	*deny, say … not*
dēferēbantur: dēferre	*bring*		
modum: modus	*measure, method*	praeeunte mē	*with me speaking (the oath) first*
an = num			
cōnfitentēs: cōnfitērī	*confess, admit*		
persevērantēs: perseverāre	*persist*	tūre: tūs	*incense*
dūcī = ad mortem dūcī		supplicārent:	
pertināciam: pertinācia	*stubbornness*	supplicāre	*make offerings*

Trāiānus Plīniō

actum quem dēbuistī, mī Secunde, in excutiendīs causīs eōrum, quī
Christiānī ad tē dēlātī fuerant, secūtus es. neque in ūniversum aliquid
cōnstituī potest. conquīrendī nōn sunt. sī dēferantur et arguantur,
pūniendī sunt. quī tamen negāverit sē Christiānum esse idque
manifestum fēcerit (id est supplicandō dīs nostrīs) veniam ex paenitentiā
impetret. sine auctōre vērō prōpositī libellī in nūllō crīmine locum habēre
dēbent. nam pessimī exemplī nec nostrī saeculī est.

5

actum: actus	*procedure*
dēlātī fuerant: dēferre	*bring, report, inform on*
in ūniversum	*as a universal rule*
cōnstituī: cōnstituere	*establish*
conquīrendī: conquīrere	*hunt out, search for*
sī dēferantur et arguantur	*if they should be brought in and proven guilty*
manifestum: manifestus	*clear*
supplicandō: supplicāre	*pray to, worship*
dīs = deīs	
veniam: venia	*pardon*
paenitentiā: paenitentia	*penitence*
impetret	*should obtain, is to obtain*
crīmine: crīmen	*charge*
pessimī exemplī	*characteristic of the worst precedent*
nostrī saeculī	*worthy of our time/age*

Roman Government and Law (Stages 37, 40, 41 & 46)

Across

1 friends/advisors of the emperor
3 men who tried inheritance cases
5 person a plaintiff first visited in a civil action
6 Latin word for a courthouse
7 the highest elected office
10 what the "C" stood for when a juror voted
12 governor of an imperial province
15 Latin term for the common people
19 Latin word for the senate
23 cases dealing with crimes of violence
24 managed public funds
25 assisted a governor in the law courts
27 Latin word for "law"
28 council that advised the emperor
29 what the "A" stood for when a juror voted

Down

2 circle of spectators who watched a court case
4 advisor/protector of the common people
5 governor of a senatorial province
8 instructions given by an emperor to a governor
9 a junior military officer
11 presided over cases concerning Roman citizens
13 were in charge of upkeep of public buildings and roads
14 junior official who helped with courts and mints
16 opinion sought from the members of the emperor's council
17 a governor from the equestrian class
18 commissions of inquiry
20 an elected official whose family had not previously held high political office
21 building where the Roman senate usually met
22 Latin word for a judge
26 numeral for the number of **tabulae** of laws

Pretend that you are the emperor.

Read the following letters to Trajan from Pliny asking for advice. Pretend you are the emperor and write, in English, your letters of response. Try for a certain tone in your replies: amused, impatient, ironic, or businesslike. Compare your letters with Trajan's actual answers which your teacher has.

A An Aqueduct for Nicomedia

in aquaeductum, domine, Nīcomēdēnsēs impendērunt HS|X̄X̄X̄|
C̄C̄C̄XVIII, quī imperfectus adhūc ōmissus, dēstructus etiam est; rūrsus in
alium ductum ērogāta sunt C̄C̄. hoc quoque relictō novō impendiō est
opus, ut aquam habeant, quī tantam pecūniam male perdidērunt.

    in prīmīs necessārium est mittī ā tē vel aquilegem vel architectum, nē   5
rursus ēveniat quod accidit. ego illud ūnum adfirmō, et ūtilitātem operis
et pulchritūdinem saeculō tuō esse dignissimam.

aquaeductum: aquaeductus	*aqueduct*
Nīcomēdēnsēs	*people of Nicomedia*
HS|X̄X̄X̄|C̄C̄C̄XVIII	*3,318,000 sesterces*
imperfectus	*unfinished, incomplete*
ōmissus = ōmissus est: ōmittere	*abandon*
dēstructus ... est: dēstruere	*destroy*
ērogāta sunt: ērogāre	*pay out (money)*
C̄C̄	*200,000 sesterces*
aquilegem: aquilex	*water-engineer*
ēveniat	*occur*
ūtilitātem: ūtilitās	*usefulness*
pulchritūdinem: pulchritūdō	*beauty*
saeculō: saeculum	*age, reign*

B Athletic Winners Lodge Complaint

āthlētae, domine, ea quae prō iselasticīs certāminibus cōnstituistī, dēbērī
sibi putant statim ex eō diē, quō sunt corōnātī; nihil enim rēferre, quandō
sint patriam invectī, sed quandō certāmine vīcerint, ex quō invehī possint.
ego contrā praescrībō "iselasticī nōmen."

ea quae	*those* (prizes) *which*
iselasticīs certāminibus	*triumphal games* (i.e. games in which winners were privileged to drive in triumph into their native towns)
cōnstituistī: cōnstituere	*award*
sunt corōnātī: corōnāre	*crown for victory*
rēferre	*concern, make a difference*
sint ... invectī: vehere	*carry in triumph*
praescrībō: praescrībere	*point out, put forward*

50

C A Sewer for Amastris

Amastriānōrum cīvitās, domine, et ēlegāns et ōrnāta habet inter
praecipua opera pulcherrimam eandemque longissimam plateam; cuius ā
latere per spatium omne porrigitur nōmine quidem flūmen, rē vērā cloāca
foedissima, ac sīcut turpis immundissimō adspectū, ita pestilēns odōre
taeterrimō. quibus ex causīs nōn minus salūbritātis quam decōris interest   5
eam contegī.

Amastriānōrum: Amastriānī	*the inhabitants of Amastris*
cīvitās	*city, city-state*
praecipua: praecipuus	*chief, special*
plateam: platea	*street*
cuius ā latere per spatium	*along the length of this*
porrigitur: porrigere	*run, extend*
turpis	*ugly, unsightly*
immundissimō: immundus	*impure, foul*
adspectū: adspectus	*sight, appearance*
pestilēns	*unhealthy*
odōre: odor	*smell, odor*
taeterrimō: taeter	*foul, offensive*
salūbritātis: salūbritās	*health*
interest: interesse	*it is in the interests* (of)
contegī: contegere	*cover over*

D The Status of Foundlings

magna, domine, et ad tōtam prōvinciam pertinēns quaestiō est dē
condiciōne et alimentīs eōrum, quōs vocant θρεπτούξ. ego audītīs
cōnstitūtiōnibus prīncipum nihil inveniēbam aut proprium aut
ūniversāle, quod ad Bīthȳnōs referrētur. cōnsulendum tē exīstimāvī.

quaestiō	*inquiry*
condiciōne: condiciō	*status, position* (i.e. slave or free)
alimentīs: alimentum	*(cost of) maintenance* (i.e. who is to pay)
θρεπτούξ (acc.)	*foundlings* (babies left at doorsteps or public places for others to find and/or rear)
cōnstitūtiōnibus: cōnstitūtiō	*imperial regulation, decision*
prīncipum: prīnceps	*emperor*
proprium: proprius	*specific, special*
cōnsulendum = cōnsulendum esse	
exīstimāvī: exīstimāre	*decide, think*

The Government of the Roman Provinces

Read pages 142–146 in your textbook and answer the following:

1 When did the Roman Empire reach its greatest extent? What province was added at that time?
2 What were two ways of acquiring new lands?
3 List four characteristics of the imperial provinces.
4 List four characteristics of a senatorial province. How might an emperor intercede in this province?
5 Describe the efforts the senate and emperor made to select suitable people for governorship.
6 Who were the **praefectī**? List two provinces under their control. Discuss why it was important to have a **praefectus** in charge of the first province. For what reason has Pontius Pilatus become so well known in the second one?
7 What was the governor's most important duty? List three ways the governor might have used troops assigned to him.
8 Describe at least two ways a Roman governor could have gained military experience before entering this office.
9 What was the governor's other main task? How did he do it? For what reason could a Roman citizen appeal to the emperor against the governor's decision?
10 What was a **iūridicus**? How did he help the governor? Who was the most famous **iūridicus** in the *Cambridge Latin Course*?
11 What were **mandāta**? Give examples of ones that Pliny might have received.
12 Explain how the Roman provincial system of taxation might have led to abuse of the provincials.
13 Describe the provincial government at the time of Trajan as seen in the correspondence of Pliny.
14 Why would Roman governors have shown **prospectus** for the provincials? How did many provincials react to the Romans and their empire?

Who wrote the letter?

Your teacher will read, in Latin, brief excerpts from the correspondence between Pliny and Trajan. Listen to the words and then check off below which man you think wrote the letter from which each excerpt is taken.

1 Pliny _____   Trajan _____   6 Pliny _____   Trajan _____

2 Pliny _____   Trajan _____   7 Pliny _____   Trajan _____

3 Pliny _____   Trajan _____   8 Pliny _____   Trajan _____

4 Pliny _____   Trajan _____   9 Pliny _____   Trajan _____

5 Pliny _____   Trajan _____   10 Pliny _____   Trajan _____

Word Power

Match the Latin word to its synonym or antonym.

1 merēre   a invenīre
2 reperīre   b īnspicere
3 vēritās   c ignis
4 cōnsuētūdō   d dignum esse
5 excutere   e mōs
6 incendium   f mendācium
7 pretiōsus   g vīlis

multās per gentēs ...

*Re-read Catullus' elegiac poem, **multās per gentēs**, page 154; study the translations in Section A; and then answer the questions in Section B. In Catullus' collection of poems, this is number 101.*

A Translations

At a brother's grave

Over the mighty world's highway,
    City by city, sea by sea,
Brother, thy brother comes to pay
    Pitiful offerings unto thee.

I only ask to grace thy bier   5
    With gifts that only give farewell,
To tell to ears that cannot hear
    The things that it is vain to tell.

And, idly communing with dust,
    To know thy presence still denied,   10
And ever mourn forever lost
    A soul that never should have died.

Yet think not wholly vain today
    This fashion that our fathers gave
That hither brings me, here to lay   15
    Some gift of sorrow on thy grave.

Take, brother, gifts a brother's tears
    Bedewed with sorrow as they fell,
And "Greeting" to the end of years,
    And to the end of years "Farewell."   20

(H. W. Garrod, 1912)

World without end

O'er many a sea, through many a tribe and nation,
    Brother, I come
To honour thee with mournful salutation
    Paid at thy tomb.
Only this final tribute may I tender   5
    In grief unheard;
Only address the dust that cannot render
    One answering word.
O thou by fate cut down, dear ghost departed

In thy first spring,   *10*
This age-old office of the broken-hearted
    Behold I bring:
A brother's tearful offerings to cover
    Thy narrow cell,
And his slow-spoken word: Farewell for ever, *15*
    Farewell, farewell.

(E. A. Havelock, 1929)

101

By strangers' coasts and waters, many days at sea,
    I came here for the rites of your unworlding,
Bringing for you, the dead, these last gifts of the living,
    And my words – vain sounds for the man of dust.
    Alas, my brother,   *5*
You have been taken from me. You have been taken from me,
    By cold Chance turned a shadow, and my pain.

Here are the foods of the old ceremony, appointed
    Long ago for the starvelings under earth:
Take them; your brother's tears have made them wet; and take *10*
    Into eternity my hail and my farewell.

(R. Fitzgerald, 1957)

101

I have come through many countries
and over many seas, brother,
to this unhappy funeral –
to give you the last gifts
of death and speak, though in vain, *5*
to your silent ashes, since fate
has taken your real self from me.
O my poor brother, taken
away from me so suddenly!
Now take these unhappy gifts,   *10*
watered with a brother's tears,
which according to the custom
of our fathers are prescribed
for funerals. And forever,
greetings, brother, and farewell.   *15*

(B. Mills, 1965)

Grief reached across the world to get me,
sadness carries me across seas and countries
to your grave, my brother,

to offer the only gift I can still give you –
words you will not hear.   5

Fortune has taken you from me. You.
No reason, nothing fair.
I didn't deserve losing you.

Now, in silence since,
as is the ancient custom of our people,   10
I say the mourner's prayer,
do the final kindness.

Accept and understand it, brother,
My head aches from crying.
Forever, goodbye.   15

(J. Rabinowitz, 1987)

B 1   What are the writers' various ways of translating the phrases **per gentēs** and **per aequora** (line 1)? Which is the translation closest to Catullus' words?

     2   Catullus states the goal of his journey as (**ad**) **hās miserās … īnferiās** (line 2). Which of the translators stay closest to Catullus' meaning, though sometimes expanding on it? Is Mills' translation "to this unhappy funeral" close enough? Rabinowitz abbreviates (**ad**) **hās miserās … īnferiās** to "your grave." Is this abbreviation helpful? How? What does it lose, however, as an expression of Catullus' feeling?

     3   Garrod takes some four lines to translate (**ut**) **mūtam nēquīquam adloquerer cinerem** (line 4); Rabinowitz takes five words. Quote both translations. Which of the two is the more effective? Why? Rabinowitz seems to take the "words" as Catullus' only gift; Garrod and the other translators take the "words" as separate from the offering. Which interpretation do you prefer? Why?

     4   Which of the translators keep Catullus' wailing apostrophe (direct address), **heu miser indignē frāter adēmpte mihī** (line 6), as direct address in English? Whose translation of the apostrophe is the most old-fashioned? Why? The saddest sounding? Why? The closest translation of Catullus' words? The shortest?

How accurate a translation for **indignē** (line 6) is Mills' "so suddenly?" Garrod's "a soul that never should have died?" Do you like Fitzgerald's repetition of "You have been taken from me?" Does Fitzgerald, by repeating this clause, deepen our awareness of Catullus' feeling or weaken it? Explain.

5   Which translator does not mention the **fortūna** (line 5) which took Catullus' brother? Which three translators name the changed, or spiritual, deceased form of Catullus' brother? What are these names? Is there any word in the Latin which justifies their naming the spiritual form of Catullus' brother? Does Catullus seem to believe in the afterlife of the dead as spirits? Is there any word in the Latin which justifies Fitzgerald's "and my pain?" Who is the only writer who translates **ipsum** in **tētē ... ipsum** (line 5)? Does **ipsum** contribute an important element to Catullus' expression of grief? If yes, what? Or are the other translators justified in ignoring it?

6   Catullus does not expressly name the "offerings" (**mūnera**, lines 7–9); which of the translators goes beyond calling them gifts, etc. and helps us see with our imagination's eye exactly what they are? Does his word picture match the visual picture printed on page 54? Which translator implies that the offerings were a prayer, not physical objects at all?

7   What are the various translations for **avē atque valē** (line 10)? Which writers do not translate **avē**? Do you agree with them that **avē** is less important than **valē**? Explain. How many of the writers keep their translations of **valē** in Catullus' position at the end of the line? What seem to be the emotional and/or logical reasons for keeping **valē** in the final position?

8   Which do you prefer for **valē**, "farewell" or "good-bye?" Why? Which word, "farewell" or "good-bye," preserves Catullus' consonance (repetition of liquid consonant "l") in lines 9–10? Do you like Havelock's echo effect for "farewell?" Does this echo effect create a feeling of reverberating emptiness? Or is it superfluous? Explain.

9   Which of the translations do you think best captures the spirit of the original poem? Give your reasons.

10 Write your own poetic translation, trying to capture the spirit of the original.

Read the following epigrams of Martial and then respond to the instructions and questions below:

tū Sētīna quidem semper vel Massica pōnis,
    Pāpyle, sed rūmor tam bona vīna negat:
dīceris hāc factus caelebs quater esse lagōnā.
    nec putō nec crēdō, Pāpyle, nec sitiō.

Sētīna = vīna Sētīna	*Setian wine* (a good wine)
Massica = vīna Massica	*Massic wine* (a good wine)
pōnis: pōnere	*serve*
negat: negāre	*deny, say that … not*
tam bona vīna negat = negat ea esse tam bona vīna	
caelebs	*widower*
quater	*four times*
lagōnā: lagōna	*bottle*
sitiō: sitīre	*be thirsty*

Eutrapelus tōnsor dum circuit ōra Lupercī
    expingitque genās, altera barba subit.

Eutrapelus tōnsor dum = dum Eutrapelus tōnsor	
circuit = circumit	
expingit: expingere	*put paint onto*
genās: gena	*cheek*
subit: subīre	*come up*

nūbere Paula cupit nōbīs, ego dūcere Paulam
    nōlō: anus est. vellem, sī magis esset anus.

nōbīs = mihi	
dūcere	*marry*
vellem	*I would be willing*

1   Re-read the other epigrams by Martial in Stage 36.

2   Considering all the epigrams you have read, write down 5 different aspects of Roman life which Martial satirizes.

3   What do you think the epigrams reveal about Martial as a person?

4   Keeping in mind the characteristic features of Martial's epigrams, write two epigrams (two to four lines each) of your own. Public figures and current events are possible targets, not a person in your school or community.

42.3 Rhythm in the Storm

A *After reviewing Metrics, pages 342–346 in your textbook, scan the following lines from page 160 in which Aeneas describes the storm.*

postquam altum tenuēre ratēs nec iam amplius ūllae

appārent terrae, caelum undique et undique pontus,

tum mihi caeruleus suprā caput adstitit imber

noctem hiememque ferēns, et inhorruit unda tenebrīs.

continuō ventī volvunt mare magnaque surgunt   5

aequora, dispersī iactāmur gurgite vāstō;

involvēre diem nimbī et nox ūmida caelum

abstulit, ingeminant abruptīs nūbibus ignēs.

excutimur cursū et caecīs errāmus in undīs.

ipse diem noctemque negat discernere caelō   10

nec meminisse viae mediā Palinūrus in undā.

trēs adeō incertōs caecā cālīgine sōlēs

errāmus pelagō, totidem sine sīdere noctēs.

quārtō terra diē prīmum sē attollere tandem

vīsa, aperīre procul montēs ac volvere fūmum.   15

B 1 Name the meter in which this passage is written.
2 In line 2, how do the rhythm and the repetition combine to help us visualize the scene?
3 Examine the 1st, 2nd, 4th, and 5th feet of line 3. What is the name for the rhythmic foot used in each? Why is that rhythmic foot appropriate in describing at what speed the storm approaches?
4 Examine the rhythmic pattern of line 4. In what way does the rhythm of the line suit the sense of the line?
5 Examine the 2nd, 3rd, and 4th feet of line 6. What is the name for the rhythmic foot used in each? What is being described here? Suggest, then, why the rhythm is effective.
6 Examine the 3rd and 4th feet of line 7. What is the technical term for the "slurring" pronunciation that occurs between these two feet? Why is it effective at this particular point in the storm?
7 Suggest how the rhythm in line 9 reinforces the meaning.
8 What does the rhythm in line 11 suggest about how Palinurus must be feeling?

42.4 Latin Poetry

Read pages 166–168 in your textbook and answer the following:

1 What form of literature did Quintilian feel that all future Roman leaders should study? What advantages did it have? What disadvantages?
2 How did Horace describe poetry in his work, *Ars Poetica*?
3 As evidenced by the graffito from Pompeii, of what was the average Roman citizen well aware and able to use?
4 What distinguishes a line of Latin poetry? How does Latin meter differ from English meter?
5 Explain how Greek poetry was closely allied to music. What did Roman poets imitate from Greek poetry?
6 What other items characterize Latin poetry besides meter?
7 How does word order affect the significance of the poet's words?
8 What three types of references would Roman poets use in their work? What demands would this make of the reader?
9 When analyzing a piece of poetry, what must we examine in addition to recognizing and labeling poetic devices?

42.5 Latin Syllables

A syllable in Latin is always centered on a vowel or diphthong, either by itself, preceded by a consonant, followed by a consonant, or sometimes preceded and followed by a consonant.

The answer to each clue is a Latin word made up of some of the syllables listed below the clues. The number of syllables in each answer is given after the English translation in parentheses. Each syllable is used once only, and every syllable is used. (If a syllable is repeated, it is written twice.)

A *After you have filled the blanks, read down the first letters of the answer words, and then the last letters. You will find the praenomen-initial and nomen of a Roman poet who wrote elegies, or love poems, followed by a quotation from one of his poems.*

60

Observe the position of the long marks when working with individual syllables, but ignore them when reading down the left and right.

Clues   *Answers*

1   I am thirsty (3)   <u>s</u> <u>i</u> - <u>t</u> <u>i</u> - <u>ō</u>

2   father (2)   __ __ - __ __ __

3   of things (2)   __ __ - __ __ __

4   everything (3)   __ __ - __ __ - __

5   almost (2)   __ __ __ - __ __

6   look! (exclamation) (1)   __ __

7   silly (masc. abl. sing.) (4)   __ __ - __ __ - __ __ - __ __

8   nevertheless (2)   __ __ - __ __ __

9   quarrel (6)   __ __ - __ - __ __ - __ __ - __ __ - __

10 bear (fem. acc. sing.) (2)   __ __ - __ __ __

11 name of Roman Stoic philosopher (3)   __ __ - __ __ - __ __

12 he had known (3)   __ __ - __ __ - __ __

13 any (fem. sing.) (2)   __ __ - __ __

14 they are taught (3)   __ - __ __ - __ __

15 he howled (4)   __ - __ __ - __ __ - __ __

16 to the priest (4)   __ __ - __ __ __ - __ __ - __ __

17 prefix **ad** before "f" (1)   __ __

18 to tell a lie (3)   __ __ __ - __ __ - __ __

19 because of this (neuter) (2 words) (2)   __ __ __ __ __

20 suddenly (3)   __ __ - __ __ __ - __ __

21 woman (acc. sing.) (3)   __ __ - __ __ - __ __ __

Syllables

a	a	af	ca	cen	cer	ci	cu	di	do	dō
ēn	fē	hoc	i	in	la	lā	lō	lu	men	men
mi	mī	nam	ne	ne	ni	nō	ob	om	pa	men
pen	rat	re	rē	rī	rī	rum	sa	sam	Se	ta
te	ter	ti	tī	tī	tur	u	ul	ur	ve	vit

B   *What are the praenomen and nomen of the Roman poet? What is the Latin quotation? What does it mean? You may wish to find a collection of translations from this poet's work and read some.*

Cēӯx et Alcyonē (Part 1)

Ceyx (pronounced SEE'-IX) was the son of the Morning Star (Lucifer), and Alcyone (pronounced AL-SIGH'-O-NEE), his wife, the daughter of the God of the Winds (Aeolus). They lived in the central Greek city of Trachis, where Ceyx was king. This was the city where Heracles spent his last days. The most famous version of the myth about this loving couple is found in Ovid's epic poem, Metamorphoses. Below are selections from Ovid's version, with prose bridge passages added. Read the passages and then answer each set of questions.

A Ceyx and Alcyone loved each other very much. One day, Ceyx decided to cross the northern Aegean sea without his wife, Alcyone, to visit Claros (in Ionia), where Apollo had an oracle. (The closer and more famous oracle at Delphi had been captured by a robber-king.) When Alcyone heard about her husband's plan, she became anxious and pleaded with him not to go.

iam potes <u>Alcyonē</u> sēcūrus abesse <u>relictā</u>?
iam via longa placet? iam sum tibi cārior absēns?
aequora mē terrent et pontī trīstis imāgō;
cum semel <u>ēmissī</u> tenuērunt aequora <u>ventī</u>,
nīl illīs vetitum est, incommendātaque tellūs   5
omnis et omne fretum: caelī quoque nūbila vexant,
excutiuntque <u>ferīs</u> rutilōs <u>concursibus</u> ignēs.
mē quoque tolle simul. certē iactābimur ūnā;
nec, nisi quae patiar, metuam, pariterque ferēmus,
quidquid erit, pariter super aequora lāta ferēmur.   10

Alcyonē	*Alcyone* (a Greek form, used here as an abl.)	concursibus: concursus	*collision*
		tolle: tollere	*take*
semel	*once*	iactābimur: iactāre	*throw, toss (about)*
nīl = nihil			
vetitum est (vetāre)	*is forbidden*	ūnā	*together*
incommendāta: incommendātus	*unprotected (supply ea)*	quae	supply **ea**
		metuam: metuere	*fear*
fretum	*ocean, sea*	pariter	*together*
nūbila: nūbilum	*cloud*	ferēmus: ferre	*carry, bear, endure*
ferīs: ferus	*wild*		
rutilōs: rutilus	*red*		

1. In lines 1–2, each of Alcyone's three questions begins with the same word. What is it? Why is this word a better choice than **nunc**, which is close in meaning? Does Alcyone expect her husband to answer these questions?
2. In lines 3–7, what is the theme of Alcyone's vividly described picture? List examples of personification in the description.
3. Why does Alcyone focus on the action of the winds? Has she experienced these herself? (Look up "Aeolus" in a handbook of mythology.)
4. In line 5, **nīl illīs vetitum est**, Alcyone expresses her meaning in a negative way. What, in English, would be the positive way?
5. Find the line among lines 3–7 which has two intertwined noun-and-adjective phrases.
6. How does the sound of **concursibus** (line 7) imitate its meaning?
7. Explain exactly the meaning of **nec, nisi (ea) quae patiar, metuam** (line 9). What would Alcyone suffer if Ceyx were to leave her behind alone? Why would she bear up better if she and he were to travel **pariter**?
8. Why do you think Alcyone emphasizes **pariter** (lines 9–10) by repeating it? What are the two words in line 8 which mean much the same thing as **pariter**?
9. **ferēmus** (line 9) and **ferēmur** (line 10) are from the same verb and have the same position in each line. But how are their meanings different?

B Alcyone's plea upsets her husband, but he will not give way to her.

tālibus Aeolidis dictīs lacrimīsque movētur
sīdereus coniūnx: neque enim minor ignis in ipsō est.
sed neque prōpositōs pelagī dīmittere cursūs
nec vult Alcyonēn in partem adhibēre perīclī;
multaque respondit timidum sōlantia pectus,   *15*
nōn tamen idcircō causam probat. addidit illīs
hoc quoque lēnīmen, quō sōlō flexit amantem:
"longa quidem est nōbīs omnis mora; sed tibi iūrō
per patriōs ignēs, sī mē modo fāta remittent,
ante reversūrum, quam lūna bis impleat orbem."   *20*

Aeolidis: Aeolis	*daughter of Aeolus (= Alcyone)*
sīdereus	*starry* (Ceyx was son of the Morning Star)
coniūnx	*husband*
pelagī: pelagus	*sea*
cursūs: cursus	*journey*
vult	understand with both **dīmittere** (line 13) and **adhibēre** (line 14)
Alcyonēn	Greek accusative form of **Alcyonē**
adhibēre	*bring*
perīclī = perīculī	
multa … sōlantia (sōlārī)	*many words to comfort*
pectus	*breast, heart*
idcircō	*on that account*
probat: probāre	*prove, make acceptable*
lēnīmen	*soothing remedy, solace*
flexit: flectere	*bend, change the mind of*
mora	*delay*
patriōs: patrius	*of one's father*
fāta: fātum	*fate*
ante … quam = antequam	*before*
reversūrum = (mē) reversūrum esse	
impleat: implēre	*fill*
orbem: orbis	*globe, sphere*

Alcyone is comforted by the thought of seeing Ceyx again within two months, but when she sees the sailboat ready to depart, she becomes frightened.

horruit Alcyonē lacrimāsque ēmīsit abortās   *21*
amplexūsque dedit, tristīque miserrima tandem
ōre "valē" dīxit, collāpsaque corpore tōtō est.

abortās: abortus	*useless, abortive*
amplexūs: amplexus	*embrace*
collāpsa … est: collābī	*collapse*

1. In line 12, an **ignis** equal to Alcyone's is said to burn in Ceyx. What does **ignis** refer to? Why is the word particularly appropriate for Ceyx?
2. What is the double bind in which Alcyone has placed Ceyx? (See lines 13–14.)
3. What is the one solace, or promise, by which Ceyx persuades Alcyone to relent from her opposition to his voyage?
4. In line 23, Alcyone, after saying good-bye, falls **corpore tōtō**. Explain whether you think these words add important information to the description of her collapse, or whether they seem added mostly to stir our feelings.

C Ceyx sets sail, but when a terrible storm comes up, his ship is battered and sinks. Ceyx swims desperately in the water.

dum natat, <u>absentem</u>, quotiēns sinit hīscere flūctus,
nōminat <u>Alcyonēn</u>, ipsīsque immurmurat undīs.   *25*
ecce super mediōs flūctūs niger arcus aquārum
frangitur, et <u>ruptā</u> mersum caput obruit <u>undā</u>.

sinit: sinere	*allow*	
hīscere	*to open one's mouth*	
flūctus	*wave*	
immurmurat: immurmurāre	*murmur to*	
super	*over*	
arcus	*arch, vault*	
obruit: obruere	*overwhelm*	

1. When does Ceyx call out the name Alcyone? In line 24, what does **absentem** mean? What Latin word does this describe? Why do you think this adjective is placed in this particular position?
2. How appropriate is the sound of the word **immurmurat** to the action described in lines 24–25?
3. In line 27, what does **mersum** mean? Why does Ovid place this word between **ruptā … undā**?

43.2 Famous Phrases

Give the meaning of the following Latin phrases:

1 mea culpa
2 numen lumen (*University of Wisconsin, Madison*)
3 forsan et haec olim meminisse iuvabit (*Vergil*)
4 in lumine tuo videbimus lumen (*Columbia University*)
5 pius Aeneas (*Vergil*)
6 scientia lumen vitae (*Texas Woman's University*)

43.3 Ausonius to His Wife

Decimus Magnus Ausonius (c. A.D. 310 – c. 393) was a poet, a politician, and a teacher of Latin literature and rhetoric at the University of Bordeaux. After reading the following poem, write a close translation of the lines. Then write your own poetic version of the whole poem.

uxor, vīvāmus ut vīximus et teneāmus
    nōmina quae prīmō sūmpsimus in thalamō:
nec ferat ūlla diēs ut commūtēmur in aevō,
    quīn tibi sim iuvenis, tūque puella mihi.
Nestore sim quamvīs prōvectior aemulaque annīs   5
    vincās Cūmānam tū quoque Dēiphobēn,
nōs ignōrēmus quid sit mātūra senectus.
    scīre aevī meritum, nōn numerāre decet.

thalamō: thalamus	*bed chamber; marriage*
ferat = faciat	
commūtēmur: commūtāre	*change*
aevō: aevum	*time; old age*
quīn	*that not*
Nestore: Nestor	*Nestor* (the oldest of the Greeks at Troy)
quamvīs	*however much*
prōvectior: prōvectus	*advanced*
aemula: aemulus	*rivaling*
Cūmānam: Cūmānus	*Cumaean*
Dēiphobēn: Dēiphobē	*Deiphobe* (the Cumaean Sibyl's name)
mātūra: mātūrus	*mature; advanced*
meritum: meritum	*merit, service*

43.4 Reverse Snake

Translate each Latin sentence into English by selecting correctly from the list of English words and phrases.

1 **sī magistrātus hoc negāvisset, eī nōn crēdidissem.**

If the officials	*had denied this*	*I would not believe*	*him.*
If the official	*were to deny this*	*I would not have believed*	*them.*

2 **sī līberī meī propter tē assiduē vituperārentur, vehementer quererer.**

If my children   were being criticized   by those sitting   next to you
If my books   had been criticized   constantly   because of you

I would be complaining   violently.
I would have been asking   for vengeance.

3 **sī hostēs copiās aggressī erunt, celerrimē fugiēmus.**

If the enemy   were to attack   the camp   we shall flee   as quickly as possible.
If the guests   attack   the troops   we would flee   very quickly.

4 **sī benignitātem tuam mereāmur, gaudeāmus.**

If we were to deserve   your kindness   we are happy.
If we deserve   your praise   we would be happy.

5 **sī fēmina fortis sepulcrum marītī tuerētur, ab omnibus nōn despicerētur.**

If the loud woman   were watching over   her buried husband
If the brave woman   is protecting   her husband's tomb

she is not deprived of   everything.
she would not be despised   by everyone.

6 **sī exercitus bona nostra dēlēvisset, domum nōn reversī essēmus.**

If the armies   had destroyed   our good people
If the army   were destroying   our property

we would not be returning   home.
we would not have returned   their gift.

7 **sī cōnsul familiam sepelīverit, diūtissimē lūgēbit.**

If the consul buries his family   he will mourn   too long.
If the consul's family is buried   he will struggle   for a very long time.

8 **sī dīvitiās optēs, deī tē rīdeant.**

If you were to desire   the gods   the gods   would laugh at you.
If you ask   riches   daylight   will return to you.

67

Latin Words Within Words

In each item, guess the two Latin words, one contained in the other.

1	d (_ _ _ _ _)	an extra in a right hand
2	h _ _ (_ _ _)	a foot at the end of a guest
3	h _ (_ _ _)	an heir gets a thing at the end
4	g _(_ _ _ _)	heavy with a bird
5	f (_ _ _ _)	loyal with the Ides
6	f (_ _ _ _ _)	a light at the end of a river
7	d _ (_ _ _ _ _) _	riches contain vices
8	c (_ _ _ _ _)	a male bear in a race
9	p _ _(_ _ _ _)	equal journey
10	d _ (_ _ _)	I destroy a lion
11	a _(_ _ _ _ _ _)	arrival with a wind
12	c _(_ _ _)	I cremate as I buy
13	l _(_ _ _ _ _ _)	a little book and pretty

fēmina fortis

In the imaginary dialogue opposite, circle the correct Latin words. Then practice the scene dramatically in pairs before performing it in class.

ūnus ex tribus mīlitibus Rōmānīs sermōnem cum Tūriā habet.

mīles: audīvimus marītum tuum ā vīcīnīs multīs (cōnspicī/cōnspicere).

Tūria: fortasse vīcīnī virum meō marītō similem cōnspexērunt. sī ego
scīrem, vōbīs (dīcerem/dīcō) ubi ille (reperīret/reperīrētur).

mīles: nōs (suspicārēmur/suspicāmur) tē (mentior/mentīrī).   5

Tūria: dī immortālēs! nōn (mentītur/mentior). ego sum mātrōna
Rōmāna; semper vērum dīcō.

mīles: tam audāx es ut (nescio/nesciam) utrum vērum ā tē
(prōnūntiātur/prōnūntiētur) an omnīnō (cēlētur/cēlātur). sī
tamen marītus tuus umquam captus (erit/est), tū quoque   10
(pūniēs/pūniēris).

mīlitēs discēdunt.

Tūria: (*sēcum cōgitāns*) tam bene marītum meum dēfendī ut neque
(superābātur/superārētur) neque (capiēbātur/caperētur). tam
callidē mentīta sum ut salūtem (adipīscēbātur/adipīscerētur).   15
nunc necesse est deīs mē ipsam adiuvāre!

43.7 Divorce and Remarriage

Read pages 186–188 in your textbook and answer the following:

1 Who is said to have been the first person in Rome to have divorced
his wife? What was the reason for the divorce?

2 Why is this unlikely to have been, in fact, the first instance of Roman
divorce?

3 List reasons that might be used in arranging a divorce.

4 Explain the difference regarding divorce between a marriage with
and without **manus**. What happened to the children of a divorced
couple?

5 What was the simplest method of obtaining a divorce?

6 What do the words **tuās rēs tibi habētō** mean? When would they
have been spoken?

7 Outline the arrangements that Zois and Antipater made in Egypt
when they were divorced.

8 What information is there on the divorce rate in Rome?

9 What does the word **dōs** mean? What would happen to this at the
time of a divorce?

10 Give one reason why remarriage was frequent in Rome.

11 What were **ūnivirae**? What religious privilege did they enjoy? What
service did they perform at a wedding?

12 How do we know that certain women (not otherwise known in
history) were **ūnivirae**?

Cēȳx et Alcyonē (Part 2)

The Story So Far

Ceyx, King of Trachis, has decided to visit the oracle of Apollo at Claros, despite the pleas of his loving wife Alcyone, who fears for his safety. On the voyage his ship is wrecked in a terrible storm and he is drowned.

D In the meantime, back home, Alcyone counts the nights until Ceyx's return. She offers incense to the gods, especially to Juno (the goddess of marriage), for his safety. But Juno eventually begins to feel the irony of the situation (Ceyx being already dead) and has a dream-figure, shaped like the ghost of poor shipwrecked Ceyx, appear to Alcyone in a dream and tell her the bad news.

> lūridus, exanimī similis, sine vestibus ūllīs
> coniugis ante torum miserae stetit: ūda vidētur
> barba virī, madidīsque gravis fluere unda capillīs. *30*
> haec ait: "agnōscis Cēȳca, miserrima coniūnx?
> an mea mūtāta est faciēs nece? respice! nōscēs,
> inveniēsque tuō prō coniuge coniugis umbram.
> nīl opis, Alcyonē, nōbīs tua vōta tulērunt.
> occidimus." *35*

lūridus	*pale* (supply "dream-ghost" as subject noun)	nece: nex	*death*
		nōscēs: nōscere	*begin to recognize*
exanimī:		opis: ops	*help, aid*
exanimis	*without breath, dead*	vōta: vōtum	*vow, prayer*
torum: torus	*bed*	occidimus = occidī:	
ūda: ūdus	*wet*	occidere	*fall, die*
unda	subject of (**vidētur**) **fluere**		
Cēȳca	*Ceyx (Greek accusative)*		

The dream-ghost of Ceyx goes on to explain pathetically:

> "nūbilus Aegaeō dēprendit in aequore nāvem
> Auster et ingentī iactātam flāmine solvit;
> ōraque nostra tuum frūstrā clāmantia nōmen
> implērunt flūctūs. nōn haec tibi nūntiat auctor
> ambiguus, nōn ista vagīs rūmōribus audīs: *40*
> ipse ego fāta tibī praesēns mea naufragus ēdō.
> surge, age, dā lacrimās lūgubriaque indue, nec mē
> indēplōrātum sub inānia Tartara mitte."

nūbilus	*cloudy, cloud-bringing*
Aegaeō: Aegaeus	*of the Aegean (Sea)*
dēprendit = dēprehendit: dēprehendere	*clutch, take hold of*

Auster	*South Wind*
flāmine: flāmen	*blast, gale*
solvit: solvere	*break up, wreck*
implērunt = implēvērunt: implēre	*fill*
auctor	*source, messenger*
ambiguus	*doubtful, vague*
ista = haec	
vagīs: vagus	*wandering, vague*
naufragus	*a shipwrecked sailor*
ēdō: ēdere	*present, proclaim*
lūgubria	*mourning clothes*
indēplōrātum: indēplōrātus	*unwept for*
Tartara	*the Underworld* (pl. of **Tartarus**)

1   Describe in your own words the appearance of Ceyx's dream-ghost (lines 28–30).
2   Re-read Stage 39, page 89, lines 7–8 about Notus, the South Wind. How is line 8, **barba … capillīs**, in the textbook similar in vocabulary and meaning to lines 29–30, **ūda … capillīs**, above? How are Notus and Ceyx's dream-ghost alike? Different?
3   How, in line 33, is **tuō coniuge** the opposite in meaning of **coniugis umbram**? How does the juxtaposition of **tuō prō coniuge coniugis umbram** emphasize the hopelessness of an exchange of Ceyx's dream-ghost for his former real body?
4   Why is **occidimus**, line 35, a more appropriate verb, in Ceyx's case, to describe his death than would have been, say, **mortuī sumus**?
5   In lines 38–39, what happened while Ceyx's mouth was calling out Alcyone's name? What is the effect of the poet's focus on Ceyx's mouth as he drowns? Compare Ovid's description of the drownings of Ceyx and of Icarus.
6   In lines 39–41, why did Ceyx's dream-ghost insist that he was the most reliable messenger of his own drowning? Is his argument valid? (Remember that the ghost was a dream-figure.) Why is **ipse** (line 41) simultaneously both a comforting and cruel word for Alcyone?
7   In lines 42–43, what were the dream-ghost's last instructions?

E The dream-ghost of Ceyx breaks into tears, as does Alcyone:

> ingemit Alcyonē, lacrimās movet atque lacertōs
> per somnum, corpusque petēns amplectitur aurās, *45*
> exclāmatque "manē! quō tē rapis? ībimus ūnā!"
> vōce suā speciēque virī turbāta sopōrem
> excutit et prīmō, sī sit circumspicit illīc,
> quī modo vīsus erat: nam mōtī vōce ministrī
> intulerant lūmen. postquam nōn invenit usquam, *50*
> percutit ōra manū laniatque ā pectore vestēs.
> "nūlla est Alcyonē, nūlla est!" ait. "occidit ūnā
> cum Cēӯce suō! sōlantia tollite verba.
> naufragus interiit."

ingemit: ingemere	*groan*	sī sit = sī (is) sit illīc quī …	
somnum: somnus	*sleep*	circumspicit:	
tē rapis: sē rapere	*rush, hurry off*	circumspicere	*look around to see (if)*
turbāta: turbātus	*confused*	laniat: laniāre	*tear*
sopōrem: sopor	*sleep*	interiit: interīre	*perish, die*

1 In lines 44–45, what did Alcyone try to do in her sleep? Did she succeed?
2 In line 46, what did Alcyone say in her sleep?
3 Why is **sopōrem excutit** (lines 47–48) a more vivid description than, say, **surgit**?
4 In lines 48–50, what did Alcyone do first after waking up? How was her action possible?
5 In lines 50–51, what did Alcyone do when she realized that what she had seen in her sleep was the ghost of her husband?
6 In line 53, what does Alcyone mean by **sōlantia tollite verba**? Is this an echo of anything earlier? (Re-read lines 15–20 in 43.1.B, page 64.)
7 Line 54 marks Alcyone's moment of realization. What was the truth she realized?

F Alcyone, mourning, runs to the harbor where she last saw Ceyx set sail.

> "hōc mihi discēdēns dedit ōscula lītore," dīcit; *55*
> prōspicit: in liquidā spatiō distante tuētur
> nescio quid quasi corpus aquā; prīmōque, quid illud
> esset, erat dubium. postquam paulum appulit unda,
> cernit: – erat coniūnx. "ille est!" exclāmat, et ūnā
> ōra comās vestem lacerat, tendēnsque trementēs *60*
> ad Cēӯca manūs, "sīc, ō cārissime coniūnx,
> sīc ad mē, miserande, redīs?" ait.

prōspicit:			cernit: cernere	*see clearly*
prōspicere	*look out*		ūnā	*at the same*
spatiō distante	*at a far distance*			*time*
tuētur: tuērī	*watch, look at*		comās: coma	*hair*
nescio quid	*something*		tendēns: tendere	*stretch out*
paulum	*a little*		miserande:	*pitiable,*
appulit: appellere	*drive, bring*		miserandus	*unfortunate*
	closer			

As Alcyone runs along the quay one of the gods (perhaps Juno) feels pity for her and changes her into a bird – a kingfisher. Transformed, Alcyone flies to her husband's floating corpse and gives it kisses with her beak. Ceyx feels the kisses. He also becomes a kingfisher.

As kingfishers (also called halcyons), Ceyx and Alcyone mate, although it is winter. They make a nest, which floats on the waves, and for seven days Aeolus (Alcyone's father) keeps his winds from disturbing the nesting pair. These are the original "halcyon days."

     coeunt fīuntque parentēs:
perque diēs placidōs hībernō tempore septem
incubat Alcyonē pendentibus aequore nīdīs.   *65*
tunc iacet unda maris: ventōs custōdit et arcet
Aeolus ēgressū, praestatque nepōtibus aequor.

coeunt: coīre	*mate*		arcet: arcēre (+ ABL)	*prevent*
hībernō: hībernus	*in the winter*		ēgressū: ēgressus	*(a) going out*
incubat:			praestat: praestāre	*show,*
incubāre (+ DAT)	*brood over*			*guarantee*
nīdīs: nīdus	*nest*		nepōtibus: nepos	*grandchild*
iacet: iacēre	*be still, be calm*			

1 Why do you think Alcyone, in her moment of realization, fled to the seashore?
2 What did Alcyone do when she realized that the corpse being washed to shore was Ceyx's (lines 58–61)?
3 Do you think it is a coincidence that Ceyx's body was washed toward Alcyone just then? Who might have directed the corpse towards the shore?
4 In what way could Ceyx be said to have kept his promise to Alcyone, made in lines 18–20 in 43.1.B, page 64?
5 Do you think his return is a comfort for Alcyone? Explain.
6 Are you comforted by the miraculous transformation of Ceyx and Alcyone into small birds? How could Ceyx be said to have been resurrected as well as transformed? Why is the floating nest, in light of the events leading up to the transformation, appropriate to the characters in the myth? How does Alcyone's unwitting forecast in lines 9–10 in 43.1.A, page 62, **pariterque ferēmus**, **quidquid erit**, **pariter super aequora lāta ferēmur**, turn out to be true?
7 Do real-life kingfishers build floating nests? Research the habits of real-life kingfishers. Which of these habits seems to have inspired the myth?
8 How many times does **ūnā** "together" appear in the passages above? Why is it such an important word in this story?

44.2 Word Power

A *Match the Latin word to the word which means approximately the same.*

1	aspicere	a	terra
2	vinculum	b	sīcut
3	velut	c	cōnspicārī
4	-ve	d	catēna
5	tellūs	e	aut
6	fēlīx	f	tenēre
7	possidēre	g	fortūnātus

B *Answer the following:*

1 Give the Latin and English for the abbreviation "viz."
2 Give the meaning of the word **scīlicet**. From what two Latin words does it come?
3 What is a "recondite" concept? Give an example.
4 Do you agree with the statement **fēlīx quī nihil dēbet**? Why or why not? Who in today's society can exemplify this statement?

Syncopated Forms

```
S  I  C  A  B  O  A  N  G  S  C  A  M  D  G
I  A  M  O  L  L  I  E  B  A  T  M  G  N  T
R  D  C  U  M  O  P  U  A  A  T  O  S  N  E
E  E  T  R  E  M  U  E  R  U  N  T  U  O  S
V  T  U  I  I  O  O  E  F  M  T  R  S  V  S
I  R  N  T  V  F  V  D  R  N  E  C  R  I  I
S  A  R  E  C  O  I  T  A  V  Q  U  Q  S  I
E  X  F  S  N  P  X  C  I  V  S  I  U  S  F
A  E  X  S  P  E  C  T  A  V  I  S  S  E  S
U  R  I  I  S  P  E  R  A  V  I  S  T  I  O
Q  U  D  V  X  P  E  R  I  I  S  S  E  T
H  N  U  A  T  R  A  N  S  I  I  S  S  E  M
O  T  E  T  N  U  R  E  U  D  A  M  S  C  S
S  U  O  O  S  B  P  V  E  H  E  U  X  E  U
A  T  E  N  U  E  R  U  N  T  X  S  M  S  T
```

Find the complete form of the following syncopated Latin verb forms in the puzzle above. The words may be vertical, diagonal, or horizontal, and either forward or backward.

COMMODASSE
DETRAXERE
EXSPECTASSES
ISSET
MADUERE
MOLLIBAT
NORAT
NOSSE
NOTASSET

PERISSE
PETIERE
QUAESIERIS
SACRIFICASSET
SPERASTI
TRANSISSEM
TENUERE
TREMUERE

Roman Pets

A *We have another sparrow poem by Catullus, in addition to the one in the textbook. Read the following and then answer the questions.*

passer, dēliciae meae puellae,
quīcum lūdere, quem in sinū tenēre,
cui prīmum digitum dare appetentī
et ācrēs solet incitāre morsūs,
cum dēsīderiō meō nitentī   5
cārum nescio quid libet iocārī
et sōlāciolum suī dolōris,
crēdō, ut tum gravis acquiēscat ardor.
tēcum lūdere sīcut ipsa possem
et trīstīs animī levāre cūrās!   *10*

quīcum = quōcum	
sinū: sinus	*lap*
prīmum digitum	*finger tip*
appetentī: appetere	*peck*
morsūs: morsus	*bite*
dēsīderiō: dēsīderium	*sweetheart*
nitentī: nitēns	*radiant*
cārum nescio quid … iocārī	*to play some sweet joke*
libet	*it pleases*
sōlāciolum	*as a small comfort*
acquiēscat	*may die down*
ardor	*anguish, passion*
possem	*I wish I were able, would that I had the chance*
trīstīs = trīstēs	
levāre	*lighten*

1 **solet** implies that the sparrow is usually with Catullus' girlfriend. What four infinitives describe what they do together (lines 2–4)?
2 What does Catullus think such time together may offer his girl (lines 5–8)?
3 What two infinitives reveal what Catullus wishes he could do?
4 Comment on the effectiveness of the word order in the last line.
5 What tone of voice do you suppose Catullus would use in lines 1–8 and then in lines 9–10: serious, playful, jealous, joking? Explain your answer.

B *Martial also wrote a poem about a pet. Read it through and then answer the questions that follow.*

Issa est passere nēquior Catullī,
Issa est pūrior ōsculō columbae,
Issa est blandior omnibus puellīs,
Issa est cārior Indicīs lapillīs,
Issa est dēliciae catella Pūblī.   *5*
hanc tū, sī queritur, loquī putābis;
sentit trīstitiamque gaudiumque,
collō nixa cubat capitque somnōs,
ut suspīria nūlla sentiantur;
hanc nē lūx rapiat suprēma tōtam, *10*
pictā Pūblius exprimit tabellā
in quā tam similem vidēbis Issam
ut sit tam similis sibī nec ipsa.
Issam dēnique pōne cum tabellā:
aut utramque putābis esse vēram, *15*
aut utramque putābis esse pictam.

nēquior: nequam	*naughty, bad*	suspīria:	
blandior: blandus	*charming*	suspīrium	*breath*
Indicīs: Indicus	*Indian*	lūx	*day*
catella	*puppy*	pictā: pingere	*paint*
collō nixa	*resting against (her master's) neck*	exprimit:	
		exprimere	*portray*
cubat: cubāre	*lie, stretch*	pōne: pōnere	*place side by side*

1 How do lines 1–4 build up suspense?
2 Translate the words that describe Issa in lines 1–5.
3 Which word is shared by Martial's poem (line 5), Catullus' poem above (line 1), and Catullus' poem in the textbook, page 218 (line 4)?
4 In lines 6–7, how does Martial make the dog seem human?
5 According to lines 10–11, why does the owner, Publius, make a painting of the dog?
6 What is the puzzle when Issa is compared with the painting (lines 14–16)?
7 Re-read lines 8–9. In the light of the rest of the poem, what additional meaning may be in the words **capit … sentiantur**?
8 Is this a poem about death or art or both? How is art said to triumph over death?
9 Martial's poem imitates Catullus' poem in the textbook only to some extent. Explain in what way it is an imitation. In theme? In structure? In vocabulary? In tone? In meter?

45.2 | Pervigilium Veneris

*The following stanzas are taken
from a much longer poem, usually
called the* Pervigilium Veneris *(an
all-night vigil in honor of Venus).
The author and date (any time from
the second century* A.D. *to the fifth
century* A.D.*) are unknown.
Different manuscripts of the poem
arrange the lines differently, but the
theme of the lyric celebration of love
and the springtime remains.*

*When you are reading the poem
aloud, stress the first syllable of
each line and then continue to
stress every other syllable.*

crās amet quī numquam amāvit, quīque amāvit crās amet:
vēr novum, vēr iam canōrum, vēr renātus orbis est;
vēre concordant amōrēs, vēre nūbunt alitēs,
et nemus comam resolvit dē marītīs imbribus.
crās amet quī numquam amāvit, quīque amāvit crās amet. *5*

Tomorrow will be the anniversary of the day when Dione (or Venus) was
first born from the waves.

flōreās inter corōnās, myrteās inter casās,
nec Cerēs nec Bacchus absunt nec poētārum deus.
tē sinente tōta nox est pervigilanda canticīs:
rēgnet in silvīs Dione! tu recēde Dēlia!
crās amet quī numquam amāvit, quīque amāvit crās amet. *10*

rūra fēcundat voluptās, rūra Venerem sentiunt;
ipse Amor, puer Dionae, rūre nātus crēditur.
hunc, ager cum parturīret, ipsa suscēpit sinū,
ipsa flōrum dēlicātīs ēducāvit osculīs.
crās amet quī numquam amāvit, quīque amāvit crās amet. *15*

78

quīque = quī + -que

canōrum: canōrus	*melodious*
renātus	*reborn*
concordant: concordāre	*be in harmony*
nemus	*wood, grove*
comam: coma	*hair, leaf*
resolvit: resolvere	*undo, loosen*
flōreās: flōreus	*flowery*
myrteās: myrteus	*of myrtle*
casās: casa	*bower, arbor*
tē = Dione	
sinente: sinere	*allow, permit*
pervigilanda: pervigilāre	*keep awake*
canticīs: canticum	*song*
recēde: recēdere	*withdraw, leave*
Dēlia: Dēlia	*Delia* (Diana, goddess of Delos)
fēcundat: fēcundāre	*fertilize*
voluptās	*sensual pleasure*
hunc = Amorem	(object of **parturīret, suscēpit, ēducāvit**)
parturīret: parturīre	*produce, bring forth*
ipsa = Dione/Venus	
sinū: sinus	*bosom*
dēlicātīs: dēlicātus	*delicate*
ēducāvit: ēducāre	*bring up*

1 Translate the first line.
2 What happens in the springtime, according to the first stanza?
3 From the second stanza list the deities who are welcome and not welcome at the festival. (Consult a reference book, if necessary.) What three details of the festival does this stanza give?
4 In the third stanza, what role do Dione and Amor (Cupid) play in nature?
5 The *Pervigilium Veneris* is a poem about love and the springtime. Explain what the writer gains or loses by the references to the gods and goddesses in these stanzas.

45.3 Obituary for a Bird

The first book of poems that Ovid is thought to have written is a collection called Amores. *The following lines are taken from one of these poems. Read the passage and answer the questions which follow.*

Funeral

psittacus, Ēōīs imitātrix āles ab Indīs,
    occidit: exsequiās īte frequenter, avēs.
īte, piae volucrēs, et plangite pectora pinnīs
    et rigidō tenerās ungue notāte genās;
horrida prō maestīs laniētur plūma capillīs;   5
    prō longā resonent carmina vestra tubā.
omnēs, quae liquidō librātis in āere cursūs,
    tū tamen ante aliōs, turtur amīce, dolē.
plēna fuit vōbīs omnī concordia vītā
    et stetit ad fīnem longa tenaxque fidēs.   10
quid tamen ista fidēs, quid rārī forma colōris,
    quid vōx mūtandīs ingeniōsa sonīs,
quid iuvat, ut datus es, nostrae placuisse puellae?
    īnfēlīx, avium glōria, nempe iacēs!
occidit ille loquāx hūmānae vōcis imāgō   15
    psittacus, extrēmō mūnus ab orbe datum.

After the Funeral

colle sub Ēlysiō nigrā nemus īlice frondet,
    ūdaque perpetuō grāmine terra viret.
sīqua fidēs dubiīs, volucrum locus ille piārum
    dīcitur, obscēnae quō prohibentur avēs.   20
psittacus hās inter nemorālī sēde receptus
    convertit volucrēs in sua verba piās.
ossa tegit tumulus, tumulus prō corpore magnus,
    quō lapis exiguus pār sibi carmen habet:
"colligor ex ipsō dominae placuisse sepulcrō;   25
    ōra fuēre mihi plūs ave docta loquī."

psittacus	*parrot*
Ēōīs: Ēōus	*eastern*
imitātrix	*imitator* (female)
Indīs: Indī	*people of India*
exsequiās īte	*attend a funeral procession*
frequenter	*in crowds*
plangite: plangere	*beat*
pinnīs = pennīs	

80

rigidō: rigidus	*stiff*
ungue: unguis	*claw, nail*
notāte: notāre	*mark*
horrida: horridus	*shivering, ruffled*
prō	*instead of*
maestīs: maestus	*sad*
laniētur: laniāre	*tear*
plūma	*feather*
resonent: resonāre	*resound*
liquidō: liquidus	*clear, bright*
librātis: librāre	*balance*
turtur: turtur	*turtle dove*
concordia	*harmony*
tenax	*steadfast*
quid (lines 11–13) = quid iuvat	*what good is [it]?*
rārī: rārus	*extraordinary*
mūtandīs: mūtāre	*change*
ingeniōsa: ingeniōsus	*talented, gifted*
ut	*as soon as*
nempe	*truly*
iacēs	*you lie low, you are dead*
loquāx	*talkative*
sub	*at the foot of*
lysiō: lysius	*Elysian*
nemus	*grove*
īlice: īlex	*holm-oak*
frondet: frondēre	*be leafy, be in leaf*
ūda: ūdus	*moist*
grāmine: grāmen	*grass*
viret: virēre	*be green*
sīqua	*if any*
dubiīs	*in doubtful things*
hās inter = inter hās	
nemorālī: nemorālis	*of woods*
convertit … in: convertere in	*turn attention to*
prō	*in comparison with, in proportion to*
exiguus	*little*
colligor: colligere	*reckon, consider*
ōra fuēre mihi	*I had a mouth*

1 What orders are given to the birds in the first six lines? What kind of substitutions must they make for human equivalents (lines 5–6)? Read lines 3 and 4 aloud. What sound effects are being used in these lines? Why?

2 Why is the turtle dove mentioned in particular?
3 Ovid asks four rhetorical questions in lines 11–13. What are these questions? Why do you think he has put the one in lines 13 and 14 last?
4 What two things are emphasized about the parrot in lines 15 and 16?
5 What place is being described in lines 17–20? (Check "Elysium" in a dictionary.) What does Ovid tell the reader about this place?
6 What effect does the parrot have here?
7 How is the parrot's tomb described?
8 The parrot is imagined as speaking its own epitaph. What does it say the tomb shows (line 25)? What does the parrot claim (quite reasonably) about its mouth in comparison with any other bird's?
9 Compare this poem with **lūgēte, ō Venerēs Cupīdinēsque**, in the textbook, page 218. In which poem is the bird itself more emphasized? How does this affect the tone of the poem?
10 How does each poem handle the topic of death? Refer to specific lines in your answer. Is one poem more serious than the other? Explain.
11 In what other respects are the poems similar or dissimilar? Consider, for instance, the role of the **puella**, and the meter of the respective poems.

45.4 Catullus and Lesbia

Read pages 229–230 in your textbook and answer the following:

1 What two very different tones could Catullus take in his poetry?
2 For what type of poetry is he chiefly famous?
3 By what name does he address the subject of many of these poems?
4 What convention was he following in using this name?
5 Explain, in detail, the connotations of this name in ancient times.
6 Who may be the actual person behind the pseudonym?
7 List at least five of the things we know about this person.
8 List at least three of the negative rumors about this person. Who is responsible for much of this uncomplimentary portrayal?
9 What two characteristics are strongly displayed in Catullan poetry?
10 What is this genre called? What was the original Greek definition of this genre?
11 What two Latin poets were most successful in adapting Greek lyric meters into Latin?
12 In what way does Latin lyric differ from Greek lyric?
13 What characteristics are shared by Greek lyric, Latin lyric, and modern lyric poetry?

45.5 Latin Bundles

*Fill the squares of the bundles below with **Latin words**. Hints in the form of English translations are given beneath each bundle.*

1   Lesbia

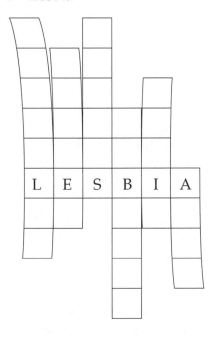

2   Īcarus

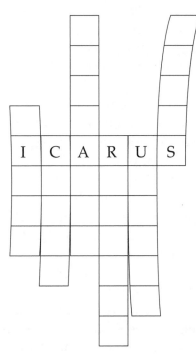

Hints: eyes (accusative plural), kisses, lips, love, name of a boyfriend, and sparrow.

Hints: name of cruel king, name of Icarus' father, name of island where labyrinth was, name of island sacred to Juno, oars, and shoulder.

45.6 Word Power: Match Play

Match the meaning to the English derivative.

1   candidate   a   open, frank
2   rupture   b   idle, indolent
3   vilify   c   a blessing
4   sensate   d   to defame, to calumniate
5   integument   e   a person seeking office
6   beatitude   f   felt by the senses
7   otiose   g   thin, unsubstantial
8   candid   h   breaking off of friendly relations
9   tenuous   i   an outer covering, e.g. skin, husk

A Different Cicero

One of the reasons for Cicero's success as an orator was the range of his eloquence. In the Pro Caelio *he was maliciously witty, but he could be equally successful in playing on the sympathy and emotions of his listeners. In an earlier attack on Verres, a rapacious Roman governor of Sicily, Cicero sympathetically described the suffering of the Sicilians, and paid tribute to the highly venerated sanctuary at Henna, sacred to Ceres. The passage below describes the beauty and sanctity of the place which Verres had sacrilegiously looted. Read the passage and answer the questions which follow.*

vetus est haec opīniō, iūdicēs, quae cōnstat ex antīquissimīs Graecōrum
litterīs ac monumentīs, īnsulam Siciliam tōtam esse Cererī et Līberae
cōnsecrātam. hoc cum cēterae gentēs sīc arbitrantur, tum ipsīs Siculīs ita
persuāsum est ut in animīs eōrum īnsitum atque innātum esse videātur.

nam et nātās esse hās in eīs locīs deās et frūgēs in eā terrā prīmum   5
repertās esse arbitrantur, et raptam esse Līberam, quam eandem
Proserpinam vocant, ex Hennēnsium nemore; quī locus, quod in mediā
est īnsulā situs, umbilicus Siciliae nōminātur. quam cum investīgāre et
conquīrere Cerēs vellet, dīcitur inflammāsse taedās eīs ignibus quī ex
Aetnae vertice ērumpunt; quās sibi cum ipsa praeferret, orbem omnem   10
peragrāsse terrārum.

Henna autem, ubi ea quae dīcō gesta esse memorantur, est locō
perexcelsō atque ēditō, quō in summō est aequāta agrī planitiēs et aquae
perennēs, tōta vērō ab omnī aditū circumcīsa atque dērēcta est; quam
circā lacūs lūcīque sunt plūrimī atque laetissimī flōrēs omnī tempore annī, 15
locus ut ipse raptum illum virginis, quem iam ā puerīs accēpimus,
dēclarāre videātur.

etenim prope est spēlunca quaedam conversa ad aquilōnem, īnfīnītā
altitūdine, quā Ditem patrem ferunt repente cum currū exstitisse
abreptamque ex eō locō virginem sēcum asportāsse, et subitō nōn longē   20
Syracūsīs penetrāsse sub terrās, lacumque in eō locō repente exstitisse;
ubi usque ad hoc tempus Syracūsānī fēstōs diēs anniversāriōs agunt
celeberrimō virōrum mulierumque conventū.

opīniō	*belief*
cōnstat	*is established*
Līberae: Lībera	*Libera (Proserpina/Persephone)*
cōnsecrātam: cōnsecrāre	*consecrate, dedicate*
cum … tum	*not only … but also*
Siculīs: Siculī	*Sicilians*
īnsitum: īnsitus	*implanted, fixed*
innātum: innātus	*innate*
frūgēs: frūgēs	*grain*
eandem: idem	*also*

Hennensium: Hennenses	*people of Henna*
nemore: nemus	*grove*
situs	*situated*
umbilicus	*navel*
investīgāre	*trace*
conquīrere	*search for*
inflammāsse = inflammāvisse: inflammāre	*kindle*
taedās: taeda	*torch*
Aetnae: Aetna	*Mt. Etna*
vertice: vertex	*summit*
praeferret: praeferre	*carry in front of*
peragrāsse = peragrāvisse dīcitur	*is said to have roamed*
gesta esse: gerī	*take place, be done*
memorantur: memorāre	*mention, relate*
perexcelsō: perexcelsus	*very high*
ēditō: ēditus	*high, lofty*
aequāta: aequāre	*make level*
planitiēs	*plain*
perennēs: perennis	*continual*
circumcīsa: circumcīdere	*cut off*
dērēcta: dērēctus	*straight up, sheer*
lūcī: lūcus	*grove*
laetissimī: laetus	*bright*
raptum: raptus	*rape, abduction*
ā puerīs	*from childhood*
etenim	*as a matter of fact*
prope	*nearby*
spēlunca	*cave*
aquilōnem: aquilō	*the north*
īnfīnītā: īnfīnītus	*endless*
altitūdine: altitūdō	*depth*
Ditem: Dis	*Dis* (Pluto/Hades)
ferunt	*they say*
exstitisse: exsistere	*appear*
abreptam: abripere	*take away by force*
asportāsse = asportāvisse: asportāre	*carry away*
Syracūsīs: Syracūsae	*Syracuse* (a city in Sicily)
usque ad	*up to*
Syracūsānī	*people of Syracuse*
fēstōs diēs anniversāriōs agunt	*observe yearly festivals*
celeberrimō: celeber	*crowded*
conventū: conventus	*gathering*

1 What ancient belief about Sicily does Cicero state at the beginning of the passage?
2 How fervently did the Sicilians believe this?
3 Cicero describes what happened at Henna, in Sicily, and says that these are tales known to Romans from childhood. Illustrate on separate paper the events and their location described in the rest of the passage. An outline of sections of the story that you should illustrate follows. Please add extra details as appropriate.

in eīs locīs	Henna (include a number of details here)
Proserpina	spēlunca
umbilicus Siciliae	sub terrās
Cerēs	lacūs
Aetna	fēstōs diēs anniversāriōs agunt
orbem terrārum peragrāsse	

4 Give examples from other religions which would coincide with the seriousness of the sacrilege that Verres had committed.

46.2 Catullus dē ōrātōribus

Read through these two poems by Catullus, and answer the questions which follow:

A The first poem is addressed to Cicero.

disertissime Rōmulī nepōtum,
quot sunt quotque fuēre, Marce Tullī,
quotque post aliīs erunt in annīs,
grātiās tibi maximās Catullus
agit pessimus omnium poēta,   5
tantō pessimus omnium poēta,
quantō tū optimus omnium patrōnus.

disertissime:
  disertus   *eloquent*
nepōtum: nepos   *descendant*
quot   *as many as*
fuēre = fuērunt
Tullī: Tullius   *Tullius*
                  (Cicero's
                  nomen)
tantō … quantō   *as much … as*
tū = tū es
patrōnus   *advocate*

1 With whom does Catullus compare Cicero in lines 1–3? What judgment does he make?
2 What judgment does Catullus make about himself in line 5?
3 Do you think Catullus really believes what he says in line 5? If he does not, what interpretation should the reader put on lines 6–7?
4 This poem is addressed to a noted expert in oratory. How has Catullus imitated rhetorical style in his poem?
5 In his *Pro Caelio*, Cicero called Clodia **omnium amīca**. Here, Catullus includes the words **omnium patrōnus**. What might he be suggesting about Cicero?
6 Suggest what might have prompted this poem.

B The second poem is a quick "snapshot" of a moment in a court case.

rīsī nescio quem modo ē corōnā,
quī cum mīrificē Vatīniāna
meus crīmina Calvus explicāsset,
admīrāns ait haec manūsque tollēns,
"dī magnī, salapūtium disertum!"   5

nescio quem: nescio quis	*someone*
corōnā: corōna	*crowd, throng, circle*
mīrificē	*wonderfully*
Vatīniāna: Vatīniānus	*against Vatinius* (the defendant)
explicāsset = explicāvisset	
salapūtium	*a little man, manikin*

1 What picture does this poem give us of Catullus' friend, Calvus?
2 What picture does it give us of the man in the audience?
3 What picture does it give us of the role oratory played in the lives of many Romans?

46.3 Latin Double Acrostic One

Fill the blanks under WORDS opposite, rows A through Z, with the Latin translations of the English CLUES. Then transfer the letters to the appropriate squares on this page. If you have worked correctly, you will be able to read (1) in the top squares, a Latin quotation, and (2) down the left margin of the WORDS, the name of the author and the title of the work from which the quotation was taken.

Treat U and V as though they were interchangeable.

1 H	2 A	▓	3 F	4 Q	5 T	6 D	7 P	▓	8 O	9 N	10 E	11 Y	▓	12 F	13 L
14 B	15 I	16 A	▓	17 C	18 I	19 G	20 L	21 S	22 Q	▓	23 I	24 L	25 G	26 Y	27 M
▓	28 A	29 R	30 T	31 I	32 E	33 R	34 D	35 Q	▓	36 D	37 E	38 N	39 V	40 F	41 H
42 I	43 T	44 H	45 S	46 X	▓	47 S	48 I	49 P	50 A	51 V	52 V	53 H	54 B	55 M	56 L
57 D	▓	58 Q	59 F	60 D	61 Z	62 L	63 V	64 B	65 G	▓	66 B	67 I	68 Y	69 M	70 D
71 G	▓	72 S	73 M	74 C	▓	75 P	76 S	77 T	78 F	79 L	80 M	▓	81 C	82 T	83 F
84 O	85 D	86 V	87 R	▓	88 P	89 A	90 B	91 Y	▓	92 C	93 M	▓	94 G	95 T	▓
96 M	97 H	98 E	99 P	100 Z	101 L	102 C	103 Z	104 B	105 Q	106 I	107 Y	108 P	109 G	110 E	▓
111 P	112 O	113 E	114 Z	115 D	▓	116 N	117 E	118 R	119 L	120 P	121 D	▓	122 A	123 P	124 X
125 C	126 Z	127 A	▓	128 H	129 C	130 T	131 Z	▓	132 V	133 I	134 Z	135 L	▓	136 L	137 O
138 S	139 R	▓	140 Y	141 Z	▓	142 I	143 D	144 M	▓	145 X	146 A	147 M	148 E	149 G	150 Z
▓	151 R	152 G	▓	153 F	154 Y	155 M	▓	156 F	157 B	158 S	159 H	160 X	161 A	162 G	▓
163 I	164 F	165 M	166 E	167 X	168 N	169 G	170 D								

CLUES

WORDS

A a province between Alps
   and Danube (accusative)

$\overline{146}$ $\overline{16}$ $\overline{161}$ $\overline{2}$ $\overline{127}$ $\overline{122}$ $\overline{28}$ $\overline{89}$ $\overline{50}$

B inn

$\overline{54}$ $\overline{64}$ $\overline{66}$ $\overline{90}$ $\overline{104}$ $\overline{14}$ $\overline{157}$

C periods of exiles (ablative)

$\overline{102}$ $\overline{74}$ $\overline{125}$ $\overline{129}$ $\overline{17}$ $\overline{81}$ $\overline{92}$

D misfortune (2 words)

$\overline{6}$ $\overline{57}$ $\overline{36}$ $\overline{115}$ $\overline{60}$ $\overline{70}$ $\overline{121}$ $\overline{85}$ $\overline{170}$ $\overline{34}$ $\overline{143}$

E you (sing.) had wandered

$\overline{10}$ $\overline{113}$ $\overline{148}$ $\overline{117}$ $\overline{37}$ $\overline{110}$ $\overline{32}$ $\overline{166}$ $\overline{98}$

F I seize (deponent)

$\overline{164}$ $\overline{3}$ $\overline{59}$ $\overline{153}$ $\overline{40}$ $\overline{78}$ $\overline{83}$ $\overline{12}$ $\overline{156}$

G wills

$\overline{25}$ $\overline{162}$ $\overline{19}$ $\overline{152}$ $\overline{149}$ $\overline{71}$ $\overline{65}$ $\overline{109}$ $\overline{94}$ $\overline{169}$

H I begin

$\overline{53}$ $\overline{44}$ $\overline{41}$ $\overline{1}$ $\overline{128}$ $\overline{159}$ $\overline{97}$

I nineteen

$\overline{31}$ $\overline{48}$ $\overline{142}$ $\overline{67}$ $\overline{23}$ $\overline{15}$ $\overline{133}$ $\overline{163}$ $\overline{18}$ $\overline{106}$ $\overline{42}$

L as soon as

$\overline{135}$ $\overline{24}$ $\overline{13}$ $\overline{79}$ $\overline{101}$ $\overline{56}$ $\overline{62}$ $\overline{136}$ $\overline{20}$ $\overline{119}$

M very great (feminine plural)

$\overline{27}$ $\overline{155}$ $\overline{96}$ $\overline{69}$ $\overline{55}$ $\overline{144}$ $\overline{165}$ $\overline{93}$ $\overline{80}$ $\overline{73}$ $\overline{147}$

N you become (singular subjunctive)

$\overline{116}$ $\overline{168}$ $\overline{9}$ $\overline{38}$

O alas!

$\overline{84}$ $\overline{8}$ $\overline{112}$ $\overline{137}$

P rhetoricians

$\overline{120}$ $\overline{88}$ $\overline{7}$ $\overline{99}$ $\overline{108}$ $\overline{75}$ $\overline{49}$ $\overline{111}$ $\overline{123}$

Q even, also

$\overline{35}$ $\overline{22}$ $\overline{58}$ $\overline{105}$ $\overline{4}$

R one and only (feminine accusative)

$\overline{151}$ $\overline{29}$ $\overline{33}$ $\overline{118}$ $\overline{87}$ $\overline{139}$

S wedding, marriage

$\overline{21}$ $\overline{76}$ $\overline{72}$ $\overline{158}$ $\overline{47}$ $\overline{138}$ $\overline{45}$

T one man (2 words) (ablative)

$\overline{130}$ $\overline{82}$ $\overline{5}$ $\overline{95}$ $\overline{30}$ $\overline{77}$ $\overline{43}$

V head (dative)

$\overline{52}$ $\overline{132}$ $\overline{39}$ $\overline{51}$ $\overline{86}$ $\overline{63}$

X honor (alternative spelling)

$\overline{124}$ $\overline{145}$ $\overline{167}$ $\overline{160}$ $\overline{46}$

Y to take revenge on

$\overline{154}$ $\overline{68}$ $\overline{91}$ $\overline{107}$ $\overline{140}$ $\overline{11}$ $\overline{26}$

Z having been pretended
   (masculine singular)

$\overline{103}$ $\overline{141}$ $\overline{150}$ $\overline{100}$ $\overline{126}$ $\overline{134}$ $\overline{114}$ $\overline{61}$ $\overline{131}$

Hints: P rhētoricus = rhetorician   X Compare the alternative spelling *arbōs* for *arbor*.

Oratory

Read pages 249–250 in your textbook and answer the following:

1 Explain the terms **quaestiōnēs** and **dē vī**.
2 Where, in Rome, did the legal procedure involving Caelius take place?
3 Who were the **praetor urbānus** and the **iūdicēs**? How were the **iūdicēs** chosen? Where did each of these groups sit?
4 Who sat near the plaintiff and the defendant? In what order did they speak?
5 What part did the **corōna** play in legal cases?
6 What choice of letters would be written on each voting tablet? What did these letters mean?
7 What roles did the **ōrātor** and **iūris cōnsultus** play in the legal system?
8 What requirements did a Roman **ōrātor** have to meet? On what did his success depend?
9 In what kind of speaking did Cicero excel? What result did this frequently have in the timing of his speeches?
10 What was the single most important reason that Cicero succeeded in politics?
11 Why was Cicero regarded as a **novus homō**?
12 What kind of orator did Cicero praise in his book, *De Oratore*?
13 Define rhetoric. Why was rhetorical training important for those involved in law courts?

47.1 The Theme of the *Aeneid*

arma virumque canō, Trōiae quī prīmus ab ōrīs
Ītaliam, fātō profugus, Lāvīnaque vēnit
lītora, multum ille et terrīs iactātus et altō
vī superum, saevae memorem Iūnōnis ob īram,
multa quoque et bellō passus, dum conderet urbem *5*
īnferretque deōs Latiō: genus unde Latīnum
Albānīque patrēs atque altae moenia Rōmae.

canō: canere	*sing of, proclaim*
profugus	*exiled*
Lavīna = Lavīnia: Lavīn(i)us	*Lavinian, of Lavinium*
iactātus = iactātus est: iactāre	*toss about*
superum = superōrum: superī	*the gods above*
passus = passus est	

A 1 According to Vergil's first two words, what are the two subjects the *Aeneid* will address?
2 Where did the hero come from, where did he go, why was it necessary for him to travel there (lines 1–3)?
3 What goddess, in particular, caused him trouble (line 4)?
4 What two things did he do which signaled the end of his travels (lines 5–6)?

B 1 The excerpt above gives the opening seven lines of the *Aeneid*. Re-read them and determine their success as an introduction. Who are the characters? What is the setting? What is the nature of the conflict? What is the theme?
2 These seven lines are filled with mythological allusions. Research the following: **Lavīn(i)a … lītora**, **Iūnōnis ob īram**, **Latiō**, **Albānī patrēs**.
3 How is the word order in line 3 effective?
4 What is the effect of the interlocking word order in line 4?
5 In line 7 how does climactic word positioning reveal the theme?

Dido reproaches Aeneas.

A *Read the following excerpt from one of Dido's central speeches in **Aeneid IV**.
The queen, learning that the Trojan fleet is being equipped for sailing, tries to
persuade Aeneas to stay:*

dissimulāre etiam spērāstī, perfide, tantum
posse nefās tacitusque meā dēcēdere terrā?
nec tē noster amor nec tē data dextera quondam
nec moritūra tenet crūdēlī fūnere Dīdō?
quīn etiam hībernō molīris sīdere classem   5
et mediīs properās Aquilōnibus īre per altum,
crūdēlis? quid, sī nōn arva aliēna domōsque
ignōtās peterēs, et Trōia antīqua manēret,
Trōia per undōsum peterētur classibus aequor?
mēne fugis? per ego hās lacrimās dextramque tuam tē   *10*
(quandō aliud mihi iam miserae nihil ipsa relīquī),
per cōnūbia nostra, per inceptōs hymenaeōs,
sī bene quid dē tē meruī, fuit aut tibi quicquam
dulce meum, miserēre domūs lābentis et istam,
ōrō, sī quis adhūc precibus locus, exue mentem.   *15*
tē propter Libycae gentēs Nomadumque tyrannī
ōdēre, īnfēnsī Tyriī; tē propter eundem
exstīnctus pudor et, quā sōlā sīdera adībam,
fāma prior. cui mē moribundam dēseris, – hospes
(hoc sōlum nōmen quoniam dē coniuge restat)?   *20*
quid moror? an mea Pygmaliōn dum moenia frāter
dēstruat aut captam dūcat Gaetūlus Iarbas?
saltem sī qua mihi dē tē suscepta fuisset
ante fugam subolēs, sī quis mihi parvulus aulā
lūderet Aenēās, quī tē tamen ōre referret,   *25*
nōn equidem omnīnō capta ac dēserta vidērer."

spērāstī = spērāvistī
posse = tē posse
nefās: nefās   *wickedness*
dēcēdere   *leave*
quīn etiam   *even worse*
hībernō: hībernus   *wintry*
molīris: molīrī   *strive to prepare*
sīdere: sīdus   *star; season*
classem: classis   *fleet*
properās: properāre   *hasten*
arva: arvum   *land*
aliēna: aliēnus   *foreign*

92

undōsum: undōsus	*surging*
quandō	*since*
hymenaeōs: hymenaeī	*wedding*
bene quid	*anything good*
quicquam dulce meum	*anything sweet in me*
miserēre: miserērī	*pity* (imperative)
lābentis: lābī	*fall*
quis … locus	*any place*
exue: exuere	*give up*
mentem: mēns	*mind; intention*
Libycae: Libycus	*of Libya* (a country of North Africa)
Nomadum: Nomadēs	*the Numidians* (a tribe in North Africa)
tyrannī: tyrannus	*ruler*
ōdēre (mē) = ōdērunt mē	
īnfēnsī (mihi sunt)	*(are) hostile (to me)*
tē propter eundem	*because of you again*
exstīnctus (est)	*is sacrificed*
sīdera: sīdus	*star; immortal fame*
moribundam: moribundus	*doomed, dying*
hospes	*stranger, guest, foreigner*
quoniam	*since*
dē coniuge	*instead of husband/spouse*
restat: restāre	*remain*
quid moror? = cūr moror?	
an mea = meane	
Gaetūlus	*of the Gaetuli* (a people in North Africa)
saltem	*at least*
qua … suscepta … subolēs	*any child born, any child conceived*
quis … parvulus … Aenēās	*any little Aeneas*
nōn equidem omnīnō	*not utterly*

B *Read the following poetic translations. Which of the translations do you think best captures the spirit of the original poem? Give your reasons.*

"Base and ungrateful! Could you hope to fly,
And undiscovered escape a lover's eye?
Nor could my kindness your compassion move,
Nor plighted vows, nor dearer bands of love?
Or is the death of a despairing queen
Not worth preventing, though too well foreseen?
E'en when the wintry winds command your stay,
You dare the tempests and defy the sea.
False as you are, suppose you were not bound
To lands unknown, and foreign coasts to sound;
Were Troy restored, and Priam's happy reign,

Now durst you tempt, for Troy, the raging main?
See, whom you fly! Am I the foe you shun?
Now, by those holy vows, so late begun,
By this right hand (since I have nothing more
To challenge, but the faith you gave before),
I beg you by these tears too truly shed,
By the new pleasures of our nuptial bed;
If ever Dido, when you most were kind,
Were pleasing in your eyes, or touched your mind,
By these my prayers, if prayers may yet have place,
Pity the fortunes of a falling race!
For you I have provoked a tyrant's hate,
Incensed the Libyan and the Tyrian state,
For you alone, I suffer in my fame,
Bereft of honour, and exposed to shame!
Whom have I now to trust, ungrateful guest?
(That only name remains of all the rest!)
What have I left? or whither can I fly?
Had you deferred, at least, your hasty flight,
And left behind some pledge of our delight;
Some babe to bless the mother's mournful sight,
Some young Aeneas to supply your place,
Whose features might express his father's face;
I should not then complain to live bereft
Of all my husband, or be wholly left."

(John Dryden, 1631–1700)

                    "And so, betrayer,
You hoped to hide your wickedness, go sneaking
Out of my land without a word? Our love
Means nothing to you, our exchange of vows,
And even the death of Dido could not hold you.
The season is dead of winter, and you labor
Over the fleet; the northern gales are nothing?
You must be cruel, must you not? Why, even,
If ancient Troy remained, and you were seeking
Not unknown homes and lands, but Troy again,
Would you be venturing Troyward in this weather?
I am the one you flee from: true? I beg you
By my own tears, and your right hand – (I have nothing
Else left my wretchedness) – by the beginnings
Of marriage, wedlock, what we had, if ever
I served you well, if anything of mine
Was ever sweet to you, I beg you pity
A falling house; if there is room for pleading

As late as this, I plead, put off that purpose.
You are the reason I am hated; Libyans,
Numidians, Tyrians, hate me; and my honor
Is lost, and the fame I had, that almost brought me
High as the stars, is gone. To whom, O guest –
I must not call you husband any longer –
To whom do you leave me? I am a dying woman;
Why do I linger on? Until Pygmalion,
My brother, brings destruction to this city?
Until the prince Iarbas leads me captive?
At least if there had been some hope of children
Before your flight, a little Aeneas playing
Around my courts, to bring you back, in feature
At least, I would seem less taken and deserted."

(Rolfe Humphries, 1894–1969)

"Unfaithful man, did you think you could do such a dreadful thing
And keep it dark? Yes, skulk from my land without one word?
Our love, the vows you made me? Do these not give you pause,
Nor even the thought of Dido meeting a painful death?
Now, in the dead of winter, to be getting your ships ready
And hurrying to set sail when northerly gales are blowing,
You heartless one! Suppose the fields were not foreign, the home was
Not strange that you are bound for, suppose Troy stood as of old,
Would you be sailing for Troy, now, in this stormy weather?
Am I the reason for going? By these tears, by the hand you gave me –
They are all I have left, to-day, in my misery – I implore you,
And by our union of hearts, by our marriage hardly begun,
If I have ever helped you at all, if anything
About me pleased you, be sad for our broken home, forgo
Your purpose, I beg you, unless it's too late for prayer of mine!
Because of you, the Libyan tribes and the Nomad chieftains
Hate me, the Tyrians are hostile: because of you I have lost
My old reputation for faithfulness – the one thing that could have
    made me
Immortal. Oh, I am dying! To what, my guest, are you leaving me
"Guest" – that is all I may call you now, who have called you
    husband,
Why do I linger here? Shall I wait till my brother, Pygmalion,
Destroys this place, or Iarbas leads me away captive?
If even I might have conceived a child by you before
You went away, a little Aeneas to play in the palace
And, in spite of all this, to remind me of you by his looks, oh then
I should not feel so utterly finished and desolate."

(C. Day Lewis, 1904–1972)

"You even hoped to keep me in the dark
As to this outrage, did you, two-faced man,
And slip away in silence? Can our love
Not hold you, can the pledge we gave not hold you,
Can Dido not, now sure to die in pain?
Even in winter weather must you toil
With ships, and fret to launch against high winds
For the open sea? Oh, heartless!
                              Tell me now,
If you were not in search of alien lands
And new strange homes, if ancient Troy remained,
Would ships put out for Troy on these big seas?
Do you go to get away from me? I beg you,
By these tears, by your own right hand, since I
Have left my wretched self nothing but that –
Yes, by the marriage that we entered on,
If ever I did well and you were grateful
Or found some sweetness in a gift from me,
Have pity now on a declining house!
Put this plan by, I beg you, if a prayer
Is not yet out of place.
Because of you, Libyans and nomad kings
Detest me, my own Tyrians are hostile;
Because of you, I lost my integrity
And that admired name by which alone
I made my way once toward the stars.
                              To whom
Do you abandon me, a dying woman,
Guest that you are – the only name now left
From that of husband? Why do I live on?
Shall I, until my brother Pygmalion comes
To pull my walls down? Or the Gaetulan
Iarbas leads me captive? If at least
There were a child by you for me to care for,
A little one to play in my courtyard
And give me back Aeneas, in spite of all,
I should not feel so utterly defeated,
Utterly bereft."

(Robert Fitzgerald, 1920–1985)

"Deceiver, did you even hope to hide
so harsh a crime, to leave this land of mine
without a word? Can nothing hold you back –
neither your love, the hand you pledged, nor even
the cruel death that lies in wait for Dido?
Beneath the winter sky are you preparing
a fleet to rush away across the deep
among the north winds, you who have no feeling?
What! Even if you were not seeking out
strange fields and unknown dwellings, even if
your ancient Troy were still erect, would you
return to Troy across such stormy seas?
Do you flee me? By tears, by your right hand –
this sorry self is left with nothing else –
by wedding, by the marriage we began,
if I did anything deserving of you
or anything of mine was sweet to you,
take pity on a fallen house, put off
your plan, I pray – if there is still place for prayers.
Because of you the tribes of Libya, all
the Nomad princes hate me, even my
own Tyrians are hostile; and for you
my honor is gone and that good name that once
was mine, my only claim to reach the stars.
My guest, to whom do you consign this dying
woman? I must say 'guest': this name is all
I have of one whom once I called my husband.
Then why do I live on? Until Pygmalion,
my brother, batters down my walls, until
Iarbas the Gaetulian takes me prisoner?
Had I at least before you left conceived
a son in me; if there were but a tiny
Aeneas playing by me in the hall,
whose face, in spite of everything, might yet
remind me of you, then indeed I should
not seem so totally abandoned, beaten."

(Allen Mandelbaum, 1926–)

47.3 Add a letter and change the meaning.

On a separate sheet of paper, translate each sentence below ignoring the blanks in those words containing them. Then add a letter in the blank so that the new word matches the English translation in parentheses, and translate the new sentence.

1 sedeō et f__ontem spectō.   (front)

2 fīlius rēgis fit pi__us.   (a pine tree)

3 Pūblius arma sua in ār__am posuit.   (strong-box)

4 anima__ gaudet.   (animal)

5 āl__ae moventur.   (dice)

6 ae__tās est molesta.   (summer)

7 in bellō mīlitēs ca__dunt.   (kill)

8 fūn__us ab omnibus videbātur.   (farm)

47.4 Epic Poetry

Read pages 269–270 in your textbook and answer the following:

1 What is historically remarkable about Greek epic poetry?
2 Of what did Greek epic originally consist? How was the poet able to sing an episode on request?
3 Aside from fragments, what Greek epics have survived? Who was the author? What was the subject matter of each epic?
4 Who were the first two epic poets writing in Latin? What was the subject matter of each of their works?
5 With what work did Latin epic reach its highest point?
6 List four common characteristics of literary epics.
7 List at least six of the conventions and technical devices used in epic poetry.
8 What makes epic poetry such a demanding genre?

Who is the husband?

Find the name of Dido's late husband (to whom she made a vow of perpetual fidelity) by filling in each set of blanks with the name of a Roman author in its English form. (The authors are all represented in Unit 4.) Then write the numbered letters in the order of their numbers in the spaces at the bottom.

1   Author of *Fables*: __ __ __ __ __ __ __ __
                                   6

2   Author of the novel *Satyricon*: __ __ __ __ __ __ __ __ __
                                                      1

3   Poet whose brother died in a far land: __ __ __ __ __ __ __ __
                                                             7

4   Poet who coined the phrase *carpe diem*: __ __ __ __ __ __
                                                         4

5   Cognomen of Ovid: __ __ __ __
                              8

6   Author of *Epigrams*: __ __ __ __ __ __ __
                                      5

7   Civil servant who wrote many letters to Trajan: __ __ __ __ __
                                                                2

8   Orator who defended Caelius against Clodia: __ __ __ __ __ __
                                                          3

Name of husband: __ __ __ __ __ __ __ __
                   1 2 3 4 5 6 7 8

Remus Redux

In the story of Romulus and Remus you have read by Livy, he refers, more than once, to multiple versions of the tales he is telling. Ovid tells yet another legend about the brothers in his work, Fasti. *Read the passage and answer the questions which follow.*

After the death of Remus

Rōmulus ut tumulō frāternās condidit umbrās,
    et male vēlōcī iusta solūta Remō,
Faustulus īnfēlīx et passīs Acca capillīs
    spargēbant lacrimīs ossa perusta suīs.
inde domum redeunt sub prīma crepuscula maestī,   *5*
    utque erat, in dūrō prōcubuēre torō.
umbra cruenta Remī vīsa est adsistere lectō,
    atque haec exiguō murmure verba loquī:

The ghost of Remus speaks

"ēn ego, dīmidium vestrī parsque altera vōtī,
    cernite sim quālis, quī modo quālis eram!   *10*
quī modo, sī volucrīs habuissem rēgna iubentīs,
    in populō potuī maximus esse meō.
nunc sum ēlāpsa rogī flammīs et inānis imāgō:
    haec est ex illō forma relicta Remō.
heu ubi Mars pater est? sī vōs modo vēra locūtī,   *15*
    ūberaque expositīs ille ferīna dedit.
quem lupa servāvit, manus hunc temerāria cīvis
    perdidit. ō quantō mītior illa fuit!
saeve Celer, crūdēlem animam per vulnera reddās,
    utque ego, sub terrās sanguinolentus eās.   *20*
nōluit hoc frāter; pietās aequālis in illō est.
    quod potuit, lacrimās mānibus ille dedit.
hunc vōs per lacrimās, per vestra alimenta rogāte,
    ut celebrem nostrō signet honōre diem."

Reaction to the ghost

mandantem amplectī cupiunt et bracchia tendunt: *25*
    lūbrica prēnsantīs effugit umbra manūs.
ut sēcum fugiēns somnōs abdūxit imāgō,
    ad rēgem vōcēs frātris uterque ferunt.
Rōmulus obsequitur, lūcemque Remūria dīxit
    illam, quā positīs iusta feruntur avīs.   *30*

ut	*when*
tumulō: tumulus	*tomb*
male vēlōcī	*fatally quick*
iusta: iusta	*funeral rites*
solūta = solūta sunt: solvere	*pay*
passīs: pandere	*spread, dishevel*
Acca = Larentia (also called Acca Larentia)	
perusta: perurere	*burn up*
sub	*close to, toward*
crepuscula: crepusculus	*twilight*
maestī: maestus	*sad, sorrowful*
utque erat	*and just as it was*
prōcubuēre: prōcumbere	*lie down*
torō: torus	*bed*
cruenta: cruentus	*bloody*
adsistere	*stand by*
exiguō: exiguus	*small*
dīmidium vestrī parsque altera vōtī	*half and the other half of your prayer (what you prayed for)*
cernite: cernere	*see, look*
modo	*just now*
volucrīs = volucrēs	
iubentīs = iubentēs	
ēlāpsa: ēlābī	*glide away from, escape*
ūbera: ūber	*teat, udder*
ferīna: ferīnus	*of a wild beast*
temerāria: temerārius	*rash*
Celer	*Celer (murderer of Remus in this version)*
reddās: reddere	*give up*
sanguinolentus	*bloody*
aequālis	*equal (to mine)*
per vestra alimenta	*by your nurture of him*
celebrem: celeber	*distinguished*
signet: signāre	*mark, designate*
lūbrica: lūbricus	*fleeting, elusive*
prēnsantīs = prēnsantēs: prēnsāre	*reach for*
obsequitur: obsequī	*obey*
lūcem: lūx	*day*
Remūria	*the Remūria (feast of Remus)*
positīs … avīs	*buried ancestors*

1   What has Romulus done for Remus at the beginning of the passage?
2   Explain the words: **male vēlōcī … Remō**.
3   Why would Faustulus and Acca (Larentia) have been particularly sad?
4   Describe the behavior of Faustulus and Acca in lines 3–6.

5   What do the words **utque erat** show about their feelings?
6   What did the ghost of Remus look like? How did he address them?
7   What contrast does Remus continue to draw for Faustulus and Acca in lines 11–14?
8   Remus refers to two stories about his earlier life in lines 15–16. What are these stories?
9   What contrast does Remus draw between **lupa** and Celer?
10 What is Remus' wish for Celer?
11 Who is **frāter** in line 21? How does Remus describe him?
12 Who are **vōs** in line 23? What does Remus ask them to do?
13 How successful are they in their request?
14 Scan lines 25 and 26. Explain how the rhythm reflects the meaning of the words.
15 Ovid's story is about relationships within a family. List the Latin words that refer to these.
16 Ovid included this story in his work, *Fasti*. Consult a Latin dictionary (under **fastus**) and write down the meaning of this word.
17 Explain the term "etiological" as it could be applied to this story.
18 Remus is a ghost, but he is also an orator. What makes his speech an effective plea?

48.2 Historiography

Read pages 287–288 in your textbook and answer the following:

1   Give the Latin name of Livy's work on Roman history.
2   What point does Livy make in the introduction to this work about the reliability of what he records?
3   Why does he include variant versions of events in his history?
4   What does **rērum gestārum memoria** mean? Explain the importance of this phrase in Livy's attitude to history.
5   Explain the word **exempla** as used by Livy.
6   Why does he think the Romans in his day are able to endure **nec vitia nec remedia**?
7   Outline the story of the Horatii and the Curiatii. What were the results of this story for Rome and Alba Longa?
8   List two works by Tacitus and one by Suetonius.
9   What attitude to writing history do Livy, Tacitus, and Suetonius share?
10 How do ancient historians differ from modern historians in
    a   their use of sources
    b   their use of direct speech?
11 How do the writings of ancient historians qualify as works of literature?

48.3 numerī Rōmanī

Write the Latin words for the following Roman numerals. Then fill in the Latin words for the numerals in the crossword puzzle.

Across

6 LXX
11 XIX
13 LXXX
15 XXX
16 CCC
17 CD
19 XX
20 L

Down

1 M
2 LX
3 DCCC
4 XVIII
5 DCCCC
7 MM
8 XL
9 DC
10 DCC
12 XC
14 C
18 CC

Latin Double Acrostic Two

Fill the blanks under WORDS opposite, rows A through ZZ, with the Latin translations of the English CLUES. Then transfer the letters to the appropriate squares on this page. If you have worked correctly, you will be able to read (1) in the top squares, a Latin quotation, and (2) down the left margin of the WORDS, the name of the author and the title of the work from which the quotation was taken.

Treat U and V as though they were interchangeable.

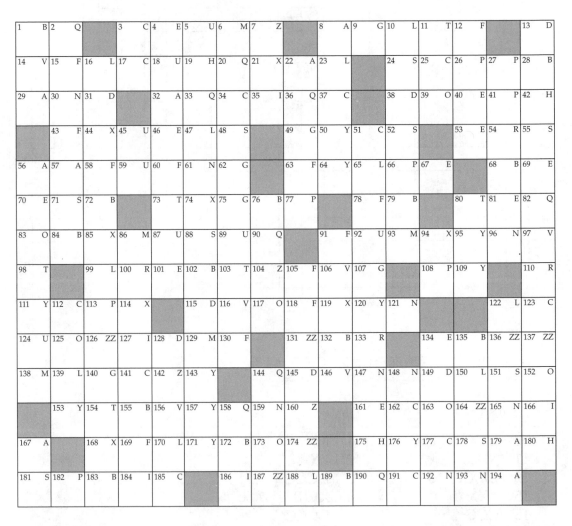

1 B	2 Q		3 C	4 E	5 U	6 M	7 Z		8 A	9 G	10 L	11 T	12 F		13 D
14 V	15 F	16 L	17 C	18 U	19 H	20 Q	21 X	22 A	23 L		24 S	25 C	26 P	27 P	28 B
29 A	30 N	31 D		32 A	33 Q	34 C	35 I	36 Q	37 C		38 D	39 O	40 E	41 P	42 H
	43 F	44 X	45 U	46 E	47 L	48 S		49 G	50 Y	51 C	52 S		53 E	54 R	55 S
56 A	57 A	58 F	59 U	60 F	61 N	62 G		63 F	64 Y	65 L	66 P	67 E		68 B	69 E
70 E	71 S	72 B		73 T	74 X	75 G	76 B	77 P		78 F	79 B		80 T	81 E	82 Q
83 O	84 B	85 X	86 M	87 U	88 S	89 U	90 Q		91 F	92 U	93 M	94 X	95 Y	96 N	97 V
98 T		99 L	100 R	101 E	102 B	103 T	104 Z	105 F	106 V	107 G		108 P	109 Y		110 R
111 Y	112 C	113 P	114 X		115 D	116 V	117 O	118 F	119 X	120 Y	121 N		122 L	123 C
124 U	125 O	126 ZZ	127 I	128 D	129 M	130 F		131 ZZ	132 B	133 R		134 E	135 B	136 ZZ	137 ZZ
138 M	139 L	140 G	141 C	142 Z	143 Y		144 Q	145 D	146 V	147 N	148 N	149 D	150 L	151 S	152 O
	153 Y	154 T	155 B	156 V	157 Y	158 Q	159 N	160 Z		161 E	162 C	163 O	164 ZZ	165 N	166 I
167 A		168 X	169 F	170 L	171 Y	172 B	173 O	174 ZZ		175 H	176 Y	177 C	178 S	179 A	180 H
181 S	182 P	183 B	184 I	185 C		186 I	187 ZZ	188 L	189 B	190 Q	191 C	192 N	193 N	194 A	

neu = nēve   *and not*
excessū: excessus   *death*
prīmordiō: prīmordium   *beginning* (of a reign)

CLUES

A wagon

B looking around (singular)

C (the) world (2 words)

D a synonym for **invenis**

E I do business (2 words)

F he had ridden (horse-back) (subj.)

G I speak (deponent)

H that (girl) of yours

I shoulders

L seventeen

M such (things)

N calmly, (in a) calm spirit (2 words)

O they cook

P intent (masculine accusative plural)

Q storm

R any (masculine ablative singular)

S worried (masculine plural)

T I bring (news)

U I have counted

V nurse

X old, ancient (dative plural)

Y you (sing.) had praised (subj.)

Z to be

ZZ you tear (up) (singular)

WORDS

32 29 179 22 57 194 8 56 167

79 84 135 189 28 68 76 102 132 155 172 1 183 72

25 17 191 51 37 34 112 123 141 162 3 177 185

145 38 128 115 149 13 31

46 81 70 67 134 53 40 101 69 161 4

12 43 169 105 63 78 91 60 15 130 118 58

75 140 49 9 107 62

19 42 180 175

166 186 184 35 127

188 170 122 47 16 65 150 10 99 139 23

138 86 93 129 6

192 30 96 121 148 159 193 165 147 61

117 152 39 173 163 125 83

77 108 113 41 26 66 182 27

2 190 158 144 36 90 20 33 82

133 54 110 100

52 48 178 55 181 24 71 88 151

154 73 80 98 11 103

87 92 5 89 59 45 18 124

14 97 106 156 146 116

74 85 94 114 168 44 21 119

153 64 95 176 111 50 157 143 120 109 171

142 104 160 7

137 126 187 131 164 136 174

Three Word Searches

Words in the search-charts below may be vertical, diagonal, or horizontal, and either forward or backward.

MARRIAGE

```
O  P  N  R  A  S  W  S  J  S
I  A  E  E  U  U  P  A  Z  I
T  T  R  W  N  T  U  X  S  L
A  E  E  F  I  I  D  G  T  A
E  R  B  L  V  R  I  U  I  I
R  F  U  A  I  A  C  N  O  T
R  A  N  M  R  M  I  A  D  P
A  M  U  M  A  I  T  M  S  U
F  I  X  E  D  Z  I  M  T  N
N  L  O  U  A  P  A  U  M  G
O  I  R  M  D  O  S  C  L  F
C  A  S  I  N  E  M  A  N  U
M  S  P  O  N  S  A  L  I  A
```

Give the Latin words for the following. Then find the words in the puzzle.

Latin word for "dowry"
The engagement ceremony
Wedding veil
Type of **cena** at a wedding
A woman who had only one husband
Ancient wedding ceremony with sacred bread
A husband
A wife
Type of marriage where the wife remains free from her husband's control
Type of marriage where the wife is under her husband's control
Latin term for "chastity"
Head of a Roman household

MYTH AND LEGEND

```
V   X   D   I   D   O   C   J   M   S
P   E   I   Y   A   Z   P   J   I   A
H   M   S   N   E   P   T   U   N   E
V   D   F   T   D   S   S   P   O   N
P   E   I   F   A   U   E   I   S   E
S   O   N   P   L   R   T   T   D   A
H   Y   R   U   U   A   O   E   W   Y
R   E   M   U   S   C   O   R   S   Q
N   O   I   R   O   I   B   O   N   H
R   C   H   Y   M   E   N   X   C   A
```

Find the names of 15 characters from myth and legend which appear in Unit 4. Identify each.

ROMAN EMPERORS

```
D   A   U   G   U   S   T   U   S   D
R   O   N   A   I   R   D   A   H   E
A   C   M   F   Q   E   N   U   G   R
C   S   U   I   D   U   A   L   C   F
S   A   T   I   T   U   S   O   L   L
A   R   I   P   R   I   S   R   A   A
P   V   T   O   A   T   A   E   V   V
V   E   R   D   J   A   P   N   T   I
D   O   P   E   A   D   S   N   I   A
F   L   A   V   N   O   E   O   R   N
```

Find the names of 8 Roman emperors which are mentioned in Unit 4.

107

48.6 What is timeless?

A *Read the following poems and songs. For each summarize the author's thought on the mortality/immortality of human creative activity, be it writing or building. Pick out at least one sentence from each that you feel best crystallizes this sentiment.*

Not marble nor the gilded monuments
Of princes shall outlive this powerful rhyme,
But you shall shine more bright in these contents
Than unswept stone besmeared with sluttish time.
When wasteful war shall statues overturn,
And broils root out the work of masonry,
Nor Mars his sword nor war's quick fire shall burn
The living record of your memory.
'Gainst death and all oblivious enmity
Shall you pace forth; your praise shall still find room
Even in the eyes of all posterity
That wear this world out to the ending doom!
　　So, till the judgement that yourself arise,
　　You live in this, and dwell in lovers' eyes.

(Shakespeare, *Sonnet 55*)

Shall I compare thee to a summer's day?
Thou art more lovely and more temperate.
Rough winds do shake the darling buds of May,
And summer's lease hath all too short a date.
Sometime too hot the eye of heaven shines,
And often is his gold complexion dimmed,
And every fair from fair sometime declines,
By chance or nature's changing course untrimmed,
But thy eternal summer shall not fade
Nor lose possession of that fair thou ow'st.
Nor shall death brag thou wander'st in his shade
When in eternal lines to time thou grow'st.
　　So long as men can breathe or eyes can see,
　　So long lives this, and this gives life to thee.

(Shakespeare, *Sonnet 18*)

Ozymandias

I met a traveler from an antique land
Who said: Two vast and trunkless legs of stone
Stand in the desert. Near them, on the sand,
Half sunk, a shattered visage lies, whose frown,
And wrinkled lip, and sneer of cold command,
Tell that its sculptor well those passions read
Which yet survive, stamped on these lifeless things,
The hand that mocked them and the heart that fed;
And on the pedestal these words appear:
"My name is Ozymandias, king of kings:
Look on my works, ye Mighty, and despair!"
Nothing beside remains. Round the decay
Of that colossal wreck, boundless and bare
The lone and level sands stretch far away.

(Percy Bysshe Shelley)

I Write The Songs

I've been alive forever,
and I wrote the very first song.
I put the words and the melodies together,
I am music
and I write the songs.
I write the songs that make the whole world sing,
I write the songs of love and special things.
I write the songs that make the young girls cry.
I write the songs, I write the songs.
My home lies deep within you,
and I've got my own place in your soul.
Now, when I look out through your eyes,
I'm young again, even though I'm very old.
I write the songs that make the whole world sing.
I write the songs of love and special things.
I write the songs that make the young girls cry.
I write the songs, I write the songs.

(Bruce Johnston)

B *Read the following Latin poem. Summarize Horace's attitude towards his poetry. Which English poem or song comes closest to expressing the same attitude?*

exēgī monumentum aere perennius
rēgālīque sitū pȳramidum altius,
quod nōn imber edax, nōn Aquilō impotēns
possit dīruere aut innumerābilis
annōrum seriēs et fuga temporum.   5
nōn omnis moriar, multaque pars meī
vītābit Libitīnam: usque ego posterā
crescam laude recēns, dum Capitōlium
scandet cum tacitā virgine pontifex.
dīcar, quā violēns obstrepit Aufidus   10
et quā pauper aquae Daunus agrestium
rēgnāvit populōrum, ex humilī potēns
prīnceps Aeolium carmen ad Ītalōs
dēdūxisse modōs. sūme superbiam
quaesītam meritīs et mihi Delphicā   15
laurō cinge volēns, Melpomenē, comam.

(Horace, *Odes III.30*)

exēgī	*I have completed, erected*
aere: aes	*bronze*
perennius: perennis	*lasting*
sitū: situs	*structure*
edax	*devouring*
impotēns	*ungovernable, wild*
dīruere	*demolish*
seriēs	*succession*
Libitīnam: Libitīna	*Libitina (goddess of funerals)*
posterā … laude recēns	*fresh in the praise of posterity*
scandet: scandere	*climb*
virgine: virgō	*the Vestal Virgin*
obstrepit: obstrepere	*thunder, roar*
Aufidus	*Aufidus (a river in Horace's native district of Apulia)*
pauper aquae	*(i.e. a land without much rainfall)*
Daunus	*Daunus (a mythical King of Apulia)*
agrestium: agrestis	*rustic, agricultural*
rēgnāvit: rēgnāre (+ GEN)	*rule over*
ex humilī potēns	*exalted from humble parentage*
prīnceps	*the first*
Aeolium carmen	*Greek meters*

110

dēdūxisse: dēdūcere   *adapt*
modōs: modus   *measure*
superbiam: superbia   *proud place*
quaesītam: quaerere   *win*
merītīs = merītīs tuīs   *by your merits*
Delphicā: Delphicus   *Delphic* (referring to Delphi, sacred
    to Apollo, god of music and poetry)

laurō: laurus   *laurel* (wreath)
cinge: cingere   *crown*
volēns   *willingly*
Melpomenē: Melpomenē   *Melpomene* (one of the Muses who
    inspired creative activity)

comam: coma   *hair, head*